Things You Never Knew or Were Told Not to Believe

Things You Never Knew or Were Told Not to Believe

Unknown Facts about Lincoln, the War, Black Bondage, and Rising Imperialism

Robert L. Price

iUniverse, Inc.
Bloomington

Things You Never Knew or Were Told Not to Believe
Unknown Facts about Lincoln, the War, Black Bondage, and Rising Imperialism

iUniverse books may be ordered through booksellers or by contacting:

iUniverse
1663 Liberty Drive
Bloomington, IN 47403
www.iuniverse.com
1-800-Authors (1-800-288-4677)

ISBN: 978-1-4697-6349-1 (sc)
ISBN: 978-1-4697-6351-4 (hc)
ISBN: 978-1-4697-6350-7 (ebk)

Printed in the United States of America

iUniverse rev. date: 02/13/2012

CONTENTS

Things You Never Knew reveals and documents facts about Abraham Lincoln that most Americans do not know and find hard to believe. It also documents untold facts about our Civil War, American Imperialism, and the biggest con on African Americans. It describes a second Civil War that began in 1865, and explains the genesis of public welfare and modern slavery with consequences that have made the Black race a perpetual under class. The author documents a current actual war on Black men and its devastation on Black families. He believes few people know that Lincoln fought to prevent the second Civil War and its tragic lasting sectional and racial hostilities. He traces a clear history of the castration of Congress and the trashing of our Constitution by our Supreme Courts and Presidents; while assuming imperialistic powers. The author cites past and present examples of misused power and force, including the war against marriage by radical feminists and foolish restrictions on personal freedoms by religions, and our government. He defends the South against current prejudice and denigration by other sections of the nation and media personalities that incite the same kind of class and political conflicts that divided the nation in the 1800s. He prescribes common sense measures to reverse the nation's course, regain lost freedoms, reduce class warfare, stop the war on the black race, and remove barriers to good racial relationships and the upward mobility of African Americans.

FORWARD

During a routine examination, my cardiologist talked about her visit to Virginia and made sarcastic remarks about Southern people. I let it pass. Several months later, I tested her knowledge of Abraham Lincoln. I asked her if Lincoln ever wanted to move all black people out of the nation. She emphatically said: "No." I put the same question to the 30 highly educated people in our Philosophical Café and Jerry, who is proud of being a Lincoln authority, angrily insisted that Lincoln did not. When you read the facts you will see how uninformed and misinformed the American public is about Lincoln, the civil war, and black freedom.

This is not another history book about Abraham Lincoln but you will see Lincoln as you have never seen him before, and may find what you see hard to believe. I will not demonize, idolize, or sanitize Lincoln. I want you to know the real Lincoln with all of his virtues and faults. This is also about our two American Civil Wars and the reasons why the second war, that began in 1865, has never ended and could be reaching a tipping point for the for the power of our federal government; with freedom hanging in the balance. It documents facts about white prejudice and racism today, and in the 1800s, that may be surprising. *Things You Never Knew* explains why the black race has become a perpetual under class and is trapped in intractable and unrecognized forms of bondage and slavery. It documents the rise of imperialism in our nation and an erosion of everyone's freedoms. There are solutions to the problems of prejudice, racism, and black and white poverty that will work better than those that have been tried for decades.

When the votes were totaled in the Presidential election in 1860, Abraham Lincoln had 1,858,200 votes, 812,500 for Breckenridge, 735,504 for Bell. The total popular vote against Lincoln was 2,824,874; a majority of 986,674 votes. Lincoln was elected in the Electoral College and did what he said he would do in his campaign speeches before the election; Southern States did what they said they would do if Lincoln was elected. I will explain how and why these things happened.

The first Civil War decisively shaped this nation and our government. The outcome of the initial conflicts between sections of the country was determined by war: the ultimate use of force. That war may have been the only way that all States could have been kept in the Union; or it may have been the worst travesty in American history. The Union prevailed but old political conflicts remain. The fights between the Federal Government and States are as hot and crucial now as they have ever been. I will present both sides as fairly and honestly as I can. The black race became free in their legal status in the 1800s but was not made truly and fully free; then or now?

I write with my maternal grandmother in mind. She was born in 1855 and was a first hand witness of the Civil War and Reconstruction and her second husband, who was twenty years older than she, was a Confederate veteran. As unlikely as it seems, I am actually a grandson of an American Civil War wife and a step-grandson of a Confederate soldier who fought in the war. I learned much from my grandmother, who lived in my home during the last ten years of her life. The Civil War is much more recent and has a stronger influence on our nation today than many of us realize. I claim the authority of documentation obtained by lengthy research and by talking with a firsthand witness.

In my personal life, I thank the Good Lord every morning for another day. Then, I tell myself that I am going to find some way to get some enjoyment and pleasure during the day and, if I can, give some pleasure to someone else. At 86, every new day is, to me, what the Louisiana Cajuns call lan-e-app (I don't know how to spell it but that is how the word is pronounced.) It means something above and beyond what is expected. If you buy a dozen eggs from a Cajun and he intentionally gives you fourteen eggs, the two extra free eggs are what the Cajuns call lan-e-app. Every new day for me is above and beyond what is expected.

For simplicity, I will be politically incorrect and will not insert a female pronoun every time I use one that is male. You will know when a pronoun refers to both genders and mankind.

I will provide a bibliography but no footnotes. If I inserted footnotes they would be more of a hindrance than help because I want to keep the text as simple as possible. I will provide the source for many, but not all, quotes because I use so many quotes, it would be cumbersome to try to insert all sources. I am indebted to all the authors of all the books that I have studied for years and have provided most of my information and many of my ideas.

I am grateful to my wife and children for their patience, understanding, and love. I want to give special thanks to Michael Tudor, a Louisiana attorney. I want to thank my wife, Clydie Mae, more than anyone else. She was my inspiration for the following poem. I am an amateur poet; as you shall see.

You and Me
When I take a look at me;
There are so many things to see.
Regrets? You bet!
I try hard to forget
But can't undo a single error;
And know each time I look at me,
It's always part of what I see.

When I take a look at me,
The hardest thing to bear
Are angry words and careless deeds
That hurt my dearest love
And children that she gave to me.

I look again and there I see
She's standing next to me.
Through it all she's by my side.
Like monkeys and angels we love and sigh
With embraces that never end.

Once more I look and see
Arms of children open wide
With earnest hugs and welcome smiles.
They say: "Old man you're not so bad!
With all your faults, you're still our dad."

From this affection and acceptance,
From folks who know me as I am,
I feel joy and warmth within me,

And know the love from hearts outside,
Like sun rays through a window,
Now makes my heart its home.

Can other souls somehow survive?
When love was never freely given
And only cold remained inside;
Or offered love could never enter
Hardened hearts with shuttered windows?

Then I look at me once more
And bless the warmth so freely given
Like waves that kiss the ocean shore
Never ending, always beginning
With someone else's love.
And give myself a great big hug.

Bob

INTRODUCTION

Some people will say that what I write is revisionist history and will not like it. If that is what they think, they are damned right. I will provide documentation to correct the incorrect politically elite and biased historians and back up everything that I write about with universally accepted quotes of Lincoln and his contemporaries. Some historians will say mean things about me but that's fair because I will say mean things about them. I will correct politically correct historians by providing recorded facts that they distort or ignore.

You may not recognize some of the quotes because I will put them in, what I believe, is their correct perspective and emphasize what some historians deemphasize; and I will reveal what they try to hide. Lincoln has been dehumanized and transformed into a god in the eyes of many people. I will not be mean or dishonest because I want you to see the human Lincoln; the man that he really was. I honor and respect him as a genius and a human.

I will not rationalize or excuse good or bad behaviors of anyone in the North or South. I will ask you to try to walk in the shoes of other people to determine for yourself if their thinking, emotions, and responses were natural and normal; whether or not they were foolish or wise. You may discover things you never knew or have been told not to believe.

This is not primarily a history; it is about people, servitude, the black and white races, the government, enemies of freedom, and the divisive second Civil War. It is about the war on black people today. I will document the war. You will discover when and how the Federal Government, the Supreme Court, and the President became super powers. You will learn when and how public welfare began. The documentation and statistics are accurately and honestly presented. *Things You Never Knew* is not a biography and it is not about God. It is about you and me and our nation. It is about black and white humans, power, slavery, drugs, governments, tyranny, and consequences of misused force. We will examine all sides of Abraham Lincoln. You must see Lincoln as he really was before you will believe any of the rest of the story. You will see facts about Honest Abe that may be hard for some people to accept as true.

Lincoln leaves no uncertainty about the reason why he waged war in Dixie. He said time and again that it was for the specific and sole purpose of saving the Union but politically correct historians still refuse to believe his plain language and insist that the primary purpose of Lincoln and the war was to free the slaves. You will see clearly how Lincoln fought hard against the idea that the purpose of the war was to free slaves. Did the end justify the means? The war set a record for carnage and atrocities. So what? We stopped those damned cotton pickers from leaving; didn't we? Almost all great nations and empires used force, coercion, and war to increase their power and expand their domain; and so did Lincoln. It was the beginning of the ongoing history of rising central power in our nation and helps explain why black bondage and racial tensions remain intractable in America? The first Civil War and the Congressional Reconstruction still exert strong influences on our culture, political and racial conflicts, and the fragile circumstances in our nation today?

There is not much in the book about the actual battles in the Civil War. They have been described and documented many times in many books and repeating them now is as useless as frosting on a crab cake. I will ask you to weigh the wisdom of the use of force and coercion to change a culture or nation as opposed to using a different kind of power and allowing a more natural evolution of society to accomplish its work. Can our world ever be completely free from hostile force, coercion, and seduction used by unscrupulous greedy people to exploit vulnerable people? I don't think so. Can we hope that our nation will never again have to suffer through another war like World War II or the first American Civil War? We can do more than just hope. We can try to find a way to eliminate, as much as possible, prejudice and racism that divides us, and make certain that that when our nation resorts to lethal military force, it will be limited to essential national defense and protection of our vital interests. Isn't that what we have always done? Of course, you jerk, don't you know those were the only reasons that the USA ever waged war? I wish that was true, but it is not.

We like to think that all of our wars have been fought only for fully justified reasons. All wars, including ours, are fought, most of all, for power and control to acquire, or hold on to, turf, territory, resources, wealth, and women for reproduction. Wars are fought to dominate or liberate people and portions of the world. We were plunged into our Civil War by ambitious politicians, radical moralists, human nature gone haywire, oversized egos, and by the conflicts of political, personal, and sectional desires—and the war has not ended.

It is natural for most people to cling to myths if the myths are pleasing. Most people also cling to perceptions of our nation's history that serves their party politics and personal interests. I will write about the precedents that Lincoln established when he became President and the lasting effects of those precedents on our Government and on the behavior of Presidents who have followed him. I will describe and document the genesis and history of escalating imperialism in America via the exaltation of the powers of our Supreme Courts, our Presidents, and the overreaching laws of our, now castrated, Congress. I will describe the motives and actions of men who were the most responsible for causing the war in 1851; motives and action that are typical of the causes of divisions and conflicts in our nation today. We are fighting the same old political war today but we, hopefully, will fight with money, votes, influence, and political power instead of bullets. I believe it is essential to know the political, cultural, and economic circumstances in the 1800s to understand the war then and now; and its actual causes.

Confederate soldiers fought, most of all, for a very simple reason; it was to defend their homes after the Union invaded Confederate territory in Virginia. After the second battle of Bull Run, General Robert E. Lee is quoted as saying: "Now, maybe they will leave us alone." In a recent television PBS documentary of the Civil War, a Union soldier asks a Confederate soldier why he is fighting and the Confederate soldier replies, "Because you are here." You invaded my home.

Rightly or wrongly Confederate soldiers believed their fight was necessary and honorable and they deserve as much respect and honor as do the heroic Union soldiers—and I will prove that their primary cause was not, I repeat, was not, to preserve slavery. (The fight did involve slavery; especially the extension of slavery into new territories.) The vast majority of white men that fought owned no slaves. They loved their State just like I love Louisiana and Colorado. When Robert E. Lee was offered the highest command of the Union Armies, he turned it down because of his loyalty to his home State. He also loved the Union and it was a hard decision. The same is true of many other military officers who had to choose between their love and loyalty to their State or the Union. Their choice did not make them virtuous or evil; it only documents the loyalty of former Union military men to their State and the pain in their choice to fight against the Union. The choice to fight for the Union or their State was often especially agonizing when it divided family members. It was as awful as a war can be because it was fratricide.

Please allow me to be angry and vitriolic for three paragraphs. I was born and lived in Louisiana until 1966; except for three years of military service during WWII. I have lived in Colorado for the last forty five years. I am often disappointed, and sometimes hurt, when I hear patent prejudice and misinformation about the South expressed by many of my good friends; friends who are highly intelligent and well educated. I am annoyed when I hear certain television personalities mock the South and I get angry when I hear my grandmother's generation derided, condemned, and grossly misrepresented. I will give illustrations. Southern people were not abominable barbarians and their reasons for fighting were not heinous; as they are painted.

The twisted contortions of our history by politically correct historians have consequences; and many of the consequences have instilled prejudice in the minds of many people. Some of the worst insults come from some television talking heads. I am including some that are not obviously anti-South but spout, what I believe, is highly biased politically motivated propaganda that offends rational and objective thinking. I realize that when you get in the mud with mudslingers you become one of them. I will take a shower after my introduction and beg for your forbearance.

It is hard to know when people who have the ear of many ordinary citizens are spouting facts or fiction. I am annoyed by the television talking head Chris Matthews, the television comedian, Bill Maher, and others like them that, in my opinion, malign the South and gin up racial, religious, and political prejudice and warfare. I abhor sarcasm and contemptuous remarks made about Southern people. We are far from perfect but no better or worse than anyone else. I haven't lived in the South since 1966 but I am proud of my Southern heritage. I am extremely proud of my maternal grandmother, and all of my family. I will stop ventilating my unpleasant emotions about TV personalities until I add a post commentary.

I will weigh the use of force to accomplish a goal, as opposed to other options, such as persuasion, education and the power of love. Force, coercion, and intimidation are common instruments of conquest and control but, also, of bondage and slavery. Perhaps the Niagara of burdensome laws flooding our nation is well intentioned, but their consequences are complicating and multiplying problems. I will ask you to consider powers that do not require law or force.

Many people do not realize how the worst consequences of our <u>two</u> Civil Wars have been on the black race in America; except for the deaths of more than 620,000 Union and Confederate troops. The Congressional Reconstruction, that Lincoln tried hard to prevent, instigated a second Civil War that has never ceased. I will also describe and document the rise of Imperialism and our vanishing freedoms. If I can add one inch to the miles of change and improvement in our nation that are needed to reduce ugly prejudice, racism, and class warfare in America and reduce the misuse of force that is eroding the freedoms of everyone, I will be happy.

Now I will take that shower; and probably need more later on. I readily admit that I am not free of prejudice but I will do my best to keep prejudice out of the rest of the story. My first chapter may be the most difficult because I may reveal a Lincoln you never knew.

CHAPTER ONE

THE MAN THE WOULD-BE COLONIZER

On March 28, 1861, Lincoln reached the breaking point. In a meeting he became visibly angry and shaken. He tore up the papers in his hands and threw them in the waste basket and ordered everyone out of the room. He complained of a "sick headache", turned white, his knees buckled and he collapsed on the floor.

Less than three months after his inauguration, the Fort Sumter crisis was weighing on Lincoln. Torrents of warnings, advice, admonitions, demands, and pleas rained on Lincoln from every direction. Lincoln threatened to use military force against seceded States during his campaign speeches and that was easy. Now, the decision of actually going to war was anything but easy. The stress and pressure on Lincoln was unrelenting and becoming unbearable and were manifested in uncommon public displays of temper. The most powerful people in Washington pounded him with loud opposing opinions. Lincoln was human and when he reached the breaking point he collapsed. Lincoln was human; not an idol, and not a God.

Early one morning, my wife and I approached the majestic marble statue of Lincoln at the end of the Washington mall. The morning was quiet and we were the only people there. My emotions are hard to describe but it was a moving experience. As we walked up the steps it was almost like walking on hallowed ground. Abraham Lincoln has been loved and idolized so profoundly, it is difficult to think of him as a man; a human being with faults and virtues just like all of us. I want you to see the human Lincoln and the kind of man that he actually was.

Psychologist, C. A. Trip, wrote a book, *The Intimate World of Abraham Lincoln* that tried to prove that Lincoln was gay. It caused quite a stir. Hundreds, perhaps thousands, of pages have been written trying to prove that Lincoln was, or was not, gay. It doesn't matter to me. I believe that is a matter of no significance or consequence to any important issue about the man and his history if Lincoln did, or did not, engage in homosexual acts. I will not waste any time talking about Lincoln's sexual preferences.

What Lincoln thought and how he felt about government and black people are, however, highly important and remain relevant. The thoughts and feelings of practically all white people in the 1800s toward black people are highly important and consequential. The South, just like the North, had its share of hot heads and hateful radicals and radicals on both sides were the primary instigators of the war; not the ordinary common people. We must know facts about the perceptions of the black race that were held by a huge majority of white people all over the nation to understand the war and its aftermath as clearly and correctly as possible. It was a rich man's war and a poor man's fight on both sides.

I will be honest with words and statements of Honest Abe that reveal his virtues and faults. Many words and statements of Lincoln that I cite have been identically recorded by honored historians, but historians have often parsed them in misleading ways. His own statements tell us about his successes and mistakes, and his good and poor judgments. You will see the rail-splitter's high ambition, his intentions, the choices he had and the decisions that he made. You will learn what Lincoln's beliefs and feelings actually were about the black race. You will see how his perceptions of black people and States affected his thinking and actions.

When I write about Lincoln's prejudice and racism, my reason is not to make moral judgments about him. My reason is to explain how racism, prejudice, and notions of white supremacy affected the thinking and behavior of practically all white people in the 1800s; including Lincoln's. We must know the real Lincoln and the truth about his contemporaries to be able to see the civil war and the black race through their eyes. We are not so blind that we cannot see the persistence of prejudice and racism today. We still have foolish arguments between historians about how much or little slavery was a cause and factor in our American Civil War and the controversies will probably never be settled.

I chose Mrs. Doris Goodwin for the most formidable living protagonists for the "politically correct" perception of Lincoln to illustrate how even her views can be shaded. She is a gracious lady who is the, or one of the, most renowned, highly honored and widely respected Lincoln historians. She is not a politically correct radical or extremists but she clearly loves, perhaps idolizes, Lincoln and her book is filled with tons and tons of praise of Lincoln and only an ounce or two of negative criticism spread here and there. She seems to want to make him as pure and blameless as she can.

For me to challenge Mrs. Goodwin is like me challenging Michael Jordan to go one on one with me on a basketball court. Her book, *Team of Rivals*, rightly deserves the high praise and acclaim that it has received. I have only one or two big beefs with her book. She includes in her book nearly all of the quotes of Lincoln that I will cite but tells us: "There is, however, the fact that armies of scholars, meticulously investigating every aspect of his life, have failed to find a single act of racial bigotry on his part." In her attempt to shield Lincoln from charges of prejudice and racism she tries to make her reader believe that the only difference between the races that Lincoln was thinking and talking about was a difference of "color". She tells us: "It is instructive, political philosopher Harry Jaffa perceptively notes that the only unequivocal statement of white supremacy Lincoln ever made was as to 'color'—the assertion of an obvious difference."

Nice try, but, in this case, you are wiggle wagging, Mrs. Goodwin. You are forthright when you tell us that Henry Jaffa acknowledged that Lincoln made an "unequivocal statement of white supremacy", but it is beneath you to imply that skin color was the only thing Lincoln was thinking of when he talked about white supremacy. You also are slyly trying to hide Lincoln from truth about his personal feelings about race when you say there is no way to penetrate his personal feelings about race. There is an easy and obvious way to penetrate Lincoln's personal feelings about race because he clearly and plainly tells us what they were; many times.

You want to make Lincoln an exception to practically all other white men in the 1800s that were chocked full and running over with prejudice and racism. If he did not harbor the same patent and well known prejudice and racism of his contemporaries, he was a strange anomaly. It is not factual for you to imply that the only differences between the races that Lincoln talked about and believed existed was "color". Did you insert the word "bigot" instead of simply using "racists" so that you can parse the meanings of your words? Why can't you let Abe be as human as his peers—and the rest of us? That should not make anyone admire and respect him any less. We do not have to be a psychoanalyst to know what Lincoln's beliefs and feeling about race were. We just have to read his words and believe that he meant what he said.

The clearest insight into Lincoln's beliefs about race is revealed in what he tells us about his desire to have the black race colonized on another continent. President Abraham Lincoln had an infallible solution for the race problem in America. It was to simply move all black people out of America and help them get settled in another country. He would provide money for them to establish their own colonies on another continent. It was called colonization. Lincoln did not want to harm the black race by this plan; he simply believed that it would be best for both races if they were separated and lived far apart from each other. He wanted and strongly promoted colonization. Newspapers published in the 1800s document the fact that nearly all white people in the North wanted a "whites only" nation and that included Lincoln. That is a simple fact that I will document with numerous written statements.

In plain language, Lincoln essentially said that he wanted to move all black people out of the country. He told Frederick Douglas and other black leaders that as long as black people stay among us they will present inevitable serious social problems. Lincoln believed that blacks and whites should never try to live together and, to attempt it would be a grievous mistake. He believed that the races are much too different to mix and live together. His words and statements are not ambiguous.

Lincoln tried to use persuasion and offers of financial assistance to convince the black race that it was in their own best interests to be separated from the white race. During the early part of the war, Lincoln invited a delegation of free black leaders to the White House to try to persuade them to accept his idea about colonizing the black race. He told them: "You and we are different races. We have between us a broader difference than exists between almost any other two races . . . . When you cease to be slaves, you are yet far removed from being placed on an equality (sic) with the white race. You are cut off from many of the advantages which the other race enjoys. (Sic) The aspiration of men is to enjoy equality with the best when free, but on this broad continent, not a single man of your race is made the equal of any man of ours . . . . It is far better for us both, therefore, to be separated." (Deporting all black people to another country would make separation of the races total and permanent.) The foremost black leader, Frederick Douglas, seemed to think that Lincoln wanted to throw his race under the bus and the leaders soundly rejected the idea. Can you imagine Lincoln standing in front of Frederick Douglas today and telling him that he can never be his equal?

I can imagine a conversation something like this; "Mister President, have you ever lived in Africa? Do you have any idea what it's like?" "Well, I grew up in a drafty one room cabin that had a dirt floor and no indoor plumbing. My second mama made dad put in a wood floor but we usually had six to eight people living in one room." "Mr. President, do you know what it's like having a tribe of hostiles on the other side of the hill who raid our tribe and try to kill us or drive us out of our land and steal our women?" "Yes I do. We had some mean Indians in our neighborhood who wanted nothing more than to kill all of us and drive us out of their land." "Mr. President, we appreciate your offer but kindly decline. We had much rather stay in this country. Even slaves have cabins to live in and clothes, and enough to eat to keep them healthy enough to work and most of them have a wife and children and most of them (not all) can stay together"

Here are some of the many recorded quotes of Lincoln's words that prove his beliefs and feelings about black people. In one of his famous debates with Stephen Douglas, Lincoln said: "I am not, nor ever have been in favor of bringing about in any way the social and political equality of the black and white races—that I am not nor ever have been in favor of making voters or jurors of negroes, nor of qualifying them to hold office, nor to intermarry with white people; and I will say in addition to this that there is a physical difference between the white and black races which I believe will forever forbid the two races living together on terms of social and political equality. (Sic) And in as much that they cannot so live, while they do remain together there must be the position of superior and inferior and I as much as any other man am (Sic) in favor of having the superior position assigned to the white race." Let me repeat Honest Abe's words. They reveal his personal feelings.

"On this broad continent, not a single man of your race is made equal of any man of ours . . . . It is far better for us both, therefore, to be separated."

"There is a physical difference between the black and white races which I believe will forever forbid the two races living together on terms of social and political equality . . . while they do remain together there must be the position of superior and inferior and I as much as any other man am in favor of having the superior position assigned to the white race." He was a Presidential candidate; can you imagine a white candidate saying that today?

Come now Mrs. Goodwin; Lincoln based his opinion of white superiority only on skin color? You cannot really believe that. What can an objective reader conclude about Lincoln's statements? We can say that Lincoln believed he was simply stating facts about racial reality in an objective manner. He probably did believe that. No one could get away with that today. Do Lincoln's statements stereotype and stigmatize the black race? My dictionary defines prejudice as: "The act or state of holding unreasonable preconceived judgments and convictions . . . an adverse judgment or opinion formed beforehand or without knowledge or examination of the facts." Was Lincoln a racist? My dictionary says that racism is: "The notion that one's own ethnic stock is superior." Of course he was prejudiced, racist, and a white supremist. It is entirely possible that when Lincoln lived, his statements about the black race were not considered prejudiced and racist.

The races must be separated and the best way to separate them is to move all black people to another continent? That is how Lincoln felt about the black race. He believed it, he preached it, and he tried hard to make it happen. Here is more proof in his words. In a message to congress on December 1, 1862, Lincoln said empathetically: "Every year since (the proposal of colonization in 1827) has added strength to the hope of its realization . . . may it indeed be realized . . . . I cannot make it better known than it already is that I *strongly favor colonization* (italics are mine)." Let's move all black people to another continent. Let's offer them money to go and get started in another country. We will pay slave owners to let them go. The USA must be a whites' only nation.

This may be something you never knew about Lincoln or were told not to believe. Mrs. Goodwin does not include the word "colonization" in her index and seems to gloss over the idea in the text of her book. Colonization was an important and actively pursued issue. Lincoln's desire to colonize all black people and his statements about black people provide an abundance of revelations about the man and his opinions of and attitude toward the black race. (Today, the Nation of Islam's leaders, like Louis Farrakhan, are the only open active advocates of colonization and the total separation of blacks and whites that I know of. Malcolm X adopted the same view early in his career but, after ten years of leadership in the Nation of Islam, he became disillusioned, left the separatists Nation and thought more like Martin Luther King. His conversion was almost certainly the reason why he was assassinated in 1965. Farrakhan has acknowledged that his preaching could have incited the assignation.)

Lincoln and other prominent leaders strongly believed that colonization was a wise idea for both races and that they could make it become a reality. Why? How could they adopt a policy that is now so foreign to all of us? In the 1800s, as always, Washington City and every part and parcel of the country was awash with inflated egos, high ambitions, political intrigue, hunger for wealth, power, and prestige, angry fighting for positions and control, and highly inflamed prejudice and racism. It will be hard for many people to believe that the Abraham Lincoln we learned about in elementary school was prejudiced and racist? Well, if we cannot see it, it is because we do not want to see it. Lincoln clearly told black leaders that the white race is superior to the black. We should not judge Lincoln too severely. He was typical of white people in every part of the budding nation. Many people think that racism was limited to the South. Lincoln genuinely wanted black people to leave the country. Antebellum plantation owners wanted the black people to remain in the country—but as slaves. A huge majority of white people in the South did not own plantations or slaves and their attitude toward colonization is unclear.

How could such a flawed man like Lincoln become one of our most idolized Presidents? He is now revered as a saint. Almost everyone believes he was one of our best Presidents. If we judge him solely by the worst carnage in American history (more than 620,000 men killed and a much greater number wounded) we must call him our worst President. The responsibility for the Civil War and its tragic lasting consequences must be borne by many people but no other one person's decision was more decisive than Lincoln's. At a crucial time, Lincoln held the ultimate decision of peace or war in his hands. Of course, if States had not seceded, he would have been spared from facing the decision. We will examine secession later.

Here are more of Lincoln's words. In a speech to a Kentucky audience that contained slave owners, he was trying to persuade the border state of Kentucky to support him when he said: "We mean to remember that you (Kentucky white people) are as good as we; that there is no difference between us except the difference of circumstances . . . We mean to marry your girls when we have a chance—*the white ones I mean.*" (Italics are mine). Would I be called racist if I made that statement?

At a State Fair in Springfield, Lincoln said: "When southern people tell us they are no more (sic) responsible for the origin of slavery, than we; I acknowledge the fact. When it is said that the institution exists; and that it is very difficult to get rid of, in any satisfactory way, I can understand and appreciate the saying. I surely will not blame them for not doing what I should not know how to do myself . . . What next? Free them, and make them politically and socially, our equals? My own feelings will not admit of this, and if mine would, we well know that those of the great mass of white people will not. Whether this feeling accords with justice and sound judgment, is not the sole question, if indeed, it is any part of it. A universal feeling, whether well or ill founded, cannot be safely disregarded." Lincoln said: "My own feelings will not admit of this, and if mine would, we well know that those of the great mass of white people will not." Slaves were not brought into America by Americans. The only reason why there were many more slaves in the South than in the North is because only plantations could employ and support large numbers of black people.

"The great mass of white people!" If you believe Lincoln and that his words were factual, he leaves no doubt that prejudice and racism was "nationwide". It was in all of the country and numerous of his contemporaries tell us that the strongest prejudice was found among common people in the North where there was little or no slavery and few black residents. In spite of all factual evidence to the contrary, people still cling to the treasured belief that Lincoln and the Northern general population went to war for the purpose of freeing the slaves. The blunt crude truth is that Lincoln, and ordinary Northerners wanted all black people out of their sight and out of the nation. Chris and Bill, did you know about that? Here are more facts.

Influential and powerful men promoted colonization. Before and after 1800, there was a more dense population of slaves in a section of New York City than any one place in the South. Most of them worked in factories and the labor unions would not admit a black person to become a member of the union and did not want blacks competing with white people in the labor market. The North had Black Code Laws before the war. Let me repeat, the North had black codes before the civil war began. Illinois, Indiana, Oregon, and other States passed legislation that prohibited black people from moving into their States. The *Revised Code of Indiana* prohibited Negroes and mulattos from coming into the state; all contracts with Negroes were null and void; any white person (such as an employer) who encouraged blacks to enter the State was subject to a fine up to $500; no Negro or mulatto could marry a white person and the act was punishable by ten years imprisonment and a fine up to $5,000. (The number of mulattos in the nation, primarily in the South, was rapidly increasing. In 1850 there were 405,523 mulattos counted in the census and the brown children were probably making their white fathers much more interested in the welfare of children that carried their genes and the black mothers who bore and cared for them.)

When Illinois, Indiana, and Oregon amended their constitutions to prohibit the emigration of blacks into their states, the amendments in public referendums were approved by more than two to one in Illinois, almost three to one in Indiana, and eight to one in Oregon. Illinois Senator Lyman Trumbull said: "There is a great aversion in the West—I know it to be so in my State—against having free Negroes come among us. Our people want nothing to do with the Negro." Northern labor unions strongly opposed abolition and the presence of black people. (Historian Victoria Bynum singles out prejudice and racism in the South as though the people in the South were the only horrible Cretans in the nation that were guilty of prejudice and racism. Of course, the South was prejudiced and racist just like the North was. I believe your prejudice, Ms. Victoria Bynum, is as obvious as water in the ocean. I will write more about her and her book later.)

Colonization was an easy sell to white men (who were not plantation owners) but it was a no-sell to the black race and was eventually abandoned. Lincoln was a genius. He should have known that black people did not want to move out of the nation. His misperceptions of black people were even worse when he was alive than the misperceptions of black people are now; and current misperceptions are a huge problem now. Colonization failed simply because the black race did not want to move out of the country and go back to Africa and Lincoln would not use force to make them leave. It was not a radical idea in the first half of the 1800s. In 1817, years before Lincoln was in power, the American Colonization Society was founded and actually established a colony in African West Liberia as a home for emigrating free black people and escaped slaves. The Society had prominent supporters and sponsored 147 ships that transported 19,000 black people to Liberia between 1817 and 1865. The Liberian government created a special committee to help the black people who moved there and our Federal Government provided financial assistance. But emigration to Liberia dwindled down to nothing and many who moved there tried to find a way to come back to America.

There is something that you may not know about Harriet Beecher Stowe, the author of *Uncle Tom's Cabin*—she favored colonization. Ms. Stowe was a powerful proponent of the abolition of slavery and a master brewer of intoxicating antislavery fervor, but she favored colonization. She had a soft spot in her heart for slaves and did not want to harm the black race but she, too, believed that separation would be best for both races. This raised the ire of black leaders toward her and they let her know about it. We find her sentiments about colonization in her famous book. She dramatizes her ideas about colonization in a way that jumps out at an unsuspecting reader from the tear stained pages of her immortal masterpiece.

Stowe's heroic protagonist was George; a brilliant runaway slave who became highly educated and successful. After George becomes successful, Stowe has him talk grandly about his decision to immigrate to Africa. George says: "I go to *my country*—my chosen, my glorious Africa—and to her, and in my heart, I sometimes apply those splendid words of prophecy: 'Whereas thou hast been forsaken and hated, so that no man went through thee; I will make thee an eternal excellence, a joy of many generations'."

Stowe has the slave, Uncle Tom; say that he feels like this nation is *not his* nation. When the benevolent slave owner, Master St Clare, prepared the papers to free Uncle Tom and told him that he is free to go wherever he wishes, Uncle Tom told his master that he did not want to leave because his master was in dire financial straits. He then said that America "is not his nation and that he has no nation." Stowe could not believe that slaves could think of America as their home. In her mind, slaves hated America and would offer their souls to the devil for a chance to board the first ship out of this evil alien nation. Stowe was mistaken, as people are today, about the condition, treatment, and feelings of many, possibly most, slaves living in this country on plantations—feelings about their nation, their living conditions, and their relationships with their masters.

Another writer tells us about a slave that did immigrate to Liberia. Matilda Skipwith, moved to Liberia and soon became miserable and homesick. She wrote to her former owner and said: "Nothing could afford me more pleasure than to visit again the scenes of childhood (on her plantation) and look on those faces that were once familiar to me." Stowe was sometimes kind in her descriptions of plantation owners and portrays some of them as benevolent and fond of their slaves. She described other plantation owners as sadistic men who beat and hanged slaves. She detested the idea of slavery and the law that made slavery possible but when she advocated colonization, Frederick Douglas no longer thought of her as a friend. Black leaders placed the horrid notions of colonization somewhere near the category of genocide.

In a recent television show, Jesse Jackson complained that black and white races in our nation are becoming more, rather than less, segregated; he calls it "resegregation". They opined about the reasons why it was happening. They never mentioned the possibility that increased segregation could often be the choice of black people who want to be with people who are the most like then and with whom they feel the most comfortable. Rev. Jackson seems to blame the government and, in some ways, he is right. Are our President and First Lady aware of increasing segregation and, if so, what do they think about it? Are they with the thinking of Jesse Jackson more than they are with radicals like Reverend Wright or Farrakhan? I have never heard Rev. Jackson curse America and I get the impression that Jesse Jackson is being snubbed by the current administration, but I could be wrong. I wonder if the President and First Lady ever make public speeches about the problems of race.

Mrs. Obama, it may help white people understand the specific reasons why you were never proud of your country before you became our First Lady if you will tell us what the specific reasons were. I believe they were normal and natural. Have you forgotten? If we can know your reasons, you can help white people learn and understand why many black people are still not proud of their country. I know that many black people have valid reasons to complain and I will describe and document some of the reasons that I know about. You have a nationwide audience to tell the nation some of the things that I will write about. I want to believe that you still loved your country even when you were not proud of it. Help open our eyes to unrecognized prejudice and how it affects all of us. How can we correct race problems if we are ignorant?

Reverend Wright exacerbated racial animosity and exploited racism when he cursed America. The worst part of it was the cheering of his audience. Is that how the majority of the black race feels today and is antagonism what America needs? Is that how he speaks to a general audience? Perhaps he could tell us things that we need to know about faults of our nation that need to changed, but it is hard to listen to a man who curses you. Wouldn't a healing balm, tolerance, and solutions for racial tensions be more helpful? Tell black and white people how we can change to make things better for everyone.

The stupid beating of a black man by policemen and the horrendous injustice that followed it in a Los Angeles courtroom released a torrent of pent up anger in black people toward policemen in a riot that randomly killed white people and looted property, and burned down a section of the city. Their behavior cannot be justified but they had valid and natural reasons to be angry.

Mrs. Obama, you can stand up for your race and educate white Americans about continuing black mistreatment with a platform that I do not have and I know you would do it in a tone much different from the inflammatory yelling of Pastor Wright. We need to know what needs to be done, practically and specifically by both races to reduce enmity and anger and improve friendship, cooperation, and goodwill between the races—and the answer is not more public welfare. I believe it is possible for racial relationships to become more beneficial than detrimental. Some callous people exploit racism for selfish and political reasons but I hope those exploiters are a minority and an exception. I know that white people can be too insensitive about race but black people can also be too sensitive to real or imagined offenses and insults. The solutions will require both races to honestly examine ourselves and our behaviors and be willing to make intelligent changes.

Lincoln's best idea was gradual emancipation. There were over three million slaves living in the midst of six million Whites in the South and only a small portion of Whites were plantation slave owners. Lincoln prophesied that an immediate emancipation for all slaves would cause the eruption of mass social disorder; and he was right. Lincoln issued a partial Emancipation Proclamation anyway during the war as a "war necessity".

Lincoln's idea of gradual emancipation was to give the slaves and the South some time and preparations for the transition of slaves from dependency on plantation owners for their living to independence, self-reliance and self-support. There were three million slaves living on plantations where white owners had the responsibility to maintain order and provide the food, clothing, shelter, and work necessary for the slaves to survive and it was unreasonable for anyone to believe that all three million could abruptly and suddenly fend for themselves and find work that would support their families. The changing economy was already making slave labor less financially advantageous for plantation owners. Within two generations machinery would replace most of the need for manual labor on the plantations and that would create an excess of unneeded workers. If it was a gradual process and if plantation owners were wise and good they could help train and prepare workers who were no longer needed for another way to make a living when they left the plantations.

If there had been no war, the children of slaves that were born in 1861 would have seen work on plantations disappearing by the time they became adults; and their children would have seen most plantation work gone by the time they became adults. There would have been no sensible reason for plantation owners to keep black people on their plantations and there would be many, many, good reasons for the owners to grant the legal status of free men to the black people who had to leave the plantations. In October, 1908, forty three years after the civil war ended, Henry Ford was manufacturing the T Model Ford and the industrial age was increasing jobs in manufacturing. Legal slavery was doomed to extinction without the war and many black people could have made a much easier and better transition to independence and self-reliance. The hopes and future of the black race was injured more than anyone else by the war, its aftermath, and the continuing second war; and I will prove it a little later.

Lincoln knew that the black race would need assistance and preparation for their adaptation to freedom and being on their own. Lincoln presaged the hard times and trouble that became a reality. He fought in vain against the Congressional Reconstruction that multiplied and intensified the problems and hardships in the South for everyone, but, especially for black men, women, and children.

There was no large exodus of black people from the South after the war. I will cite the 1860 and 1870 censuses to show that the number of black people in Southern States increased during that time. Most had to remain on plantations for work and a living.

Lincoln was a man; a human being who was much the same as you and me and his contemporaries. We do Abe an injustice when we idolize him and make him a god and don't allow him to be human—and cannot accept and respect him with human faults.

CHAPTER TWO

DECLARATIONS OF WAR

In 1856 Lincoln was on the campaign trail. His speech to the Republican Convention in Bloomington began softly and gradually rose in tempo until Lincoln was on fire. Excitement in the audience rose with his tempo until the audience was on their feet. "We will say to the Southern disunionists (sic), we want go out of the Union and you <u>shan't</u>" The delegates were standing, cheering, and in a frenzy. Men threw their hats in the air. One reporter said that many words came from Lincoln that day of "daring and equally high and challenging import." Bill Herndon said: "He's been baptized." Lincoln has gone radical. The radical leaders of the Northern Republicans cheered Lincoln's declarations of war. One historian gave his book the title *Mr. Lincoln Goes to War* and was called vile names by other historians. I am now too old to care what anyone calls me.

Before he was elected President, Lincoln clearly warned Southern States that he would use force to prevent them from leaving the Union; or to make them return to the Union if they left. What did he mean by force? He left no doubt about what he meant. Lincoln, catering to the more radical element of the Republican part, took the hard line. He knew that Southern States said they would secede if he was elected but this knowledge did not soften his campaign speeches. Lincoln made himself the war and force candidate.

Numerous historians tell us that: "At Galena on July 23, 1856, Lincoln went radical." In his speech at Galena, he brandished, for the first time, the naked might and force of the Union and directly threatened the South. He said: "The Union, in any event, won't be dissolved. We don't want to dissolve it, and if you attempt it, *we won't let you*. With the purse and sword, the army, navy, and treasury in our hands, and at our command, you *couldn't do it*. This government would be very weak, indeed, if a majority, with a well disciplined army and navy, and

14

a well-filled treasury, could not preserve itself, when attacked by an unarmed, undisciplined, and unorganized minority. All this talk about the dissolution of the Union is humbug—nothing but folly. We *won't* dissolve the Union and *you shan't*." His toast at a Chicago banquet was to: "The Union—the North will maintain it—the South will not depart there from." (Did Lincoln have any credible evidence or valid reason to believe that the South had any intentions of attacking the Union? Of course, he did not. Lincoln was rabble rousing to arouse hostile emotions and win over radical Republicans.)

"With a well disciplined army and navy, and a well-filled treasury in our hand" we will not let you. There is nothing ambiguous about Lincoln's meaning of force. He said that he would use the army and navy to wage war against seceded States. With these and other statements, Lincoln brashly stated that he would use "the purse and the sword" to force States to do his bidding. He laid down the predicate for war and uttered dire declarations of war. Let me repeat; as early as 1856, Lincoln declared war against any State that seceded. Did he frighten the South? He certainly did because Southerners believed that he meant what he said—and they were right.

When Lincoln was on the campaign trail to become President he knew that Southern States were seriously talking about seceding from the Union if he became President. His words were belligerent. Southern States intentions of seceding were not "mere humbug" or meaningless threats. Those States waited anxiously for the outcome of the election because they also meant what they said about seceding if he was elected.

Candidate Stephen Douglas was also on the campaign trail with liberal ideas and a peace platform. He was Lincoln's most formidable political and ideological opponent. Douglas accused Lincoln of talking like a reckless political opportunist and warned the nation that the inevitable consequences of Lincoln's words and threats would be war. He said: "Mr. Lincoln advocates boldly and clearly a war of sections, a war of the North against the South, of the Free States against the slave States—a war of extermination—to be continued relentlessly until the one or the other shall be subdued." Douglas was right. The warning of Douglas was dire but he knew, and Lincoln should have known, what the consequences of his bellicose rhetoric would be. The hot and dangerous tinderbox of passions in play was ready to explode. Douglas made a factual tragic prediction of the worst and deadliest war that Americans would ever suffer. He knew that the combustible emotions on both sides had a short fuse and the elected President would hold the match.

Lincoln repeated and expounded on his predicate for war in a speech on June 16, 1858, "A house divided against itself (sic) cannot stand. I believe this government cannot endure permanently half slave and half free. I do not expect the Union to be dissolved—I do not expect the house to fall—but I do expect it will cease to be divided. It will become *all* one thing or *all* the other." The die was cast.

Lincoln included in his inaugural address a paragraph that anticipated civil war but sought to place blame on the South if a war ensued and to give the Union justification for their aggression. "In your hands, my dissatisfied (sic) fellow countrymen, and not in mine, is the momentous issue of civil war. The government will not assail you. You can have no conflict without being yourselves the aggressors. You have no oath registered in Heaven to destroy the government while I have the most solemn one to preserve, protect, and defend it." (Meaning my presidential oath comes from heaven but yours doesn't.) In plain words, Lincoln asserts that he is on a "heavenly" mission for God. How often have we heard that claim during the long history of war and human beings?

The Baltimore *Sun* said: "It assumes despotic authority, and intimates the design to exercise that authority to any extent of war and bloodshed. If it means what it says, it is the knell and requiem of the Union, and the death of hope."

The Richmond *Enquirer* said it was: "The cool, unimpassioned, deliberate language of the fanatic . . . Sectional war awaits only the signal gun."

The Baltimore *Exchange* said: "The measures of Mr. Lincoln mean war." Maryland was a border State that did not choose a side.

Lincoln said what he meant and he meant what he said. His words cannot be parsed, rationalized, or colored to mean anything but a declaration of war. Only a willful disregard for facts and truth can make them mean anything else. I don't know if anyone else who has written about Lincoln has acknowledged and admitted that Honest Abe bluntly declared war against States before he was elected and carried out his intention when he became President. Of course, he would prefer the States to stay in, or return to, the Union without a war, but if they didn't, he intended to go to war; he insisted on going to war, and he waged war.

The South knew exactly what Lincoln meant when he threatened them with the use of force. They knew he was talking about a military war and became frightened and angry. The South rightly knew that war would be costly and bloody and they had no guarantee that they could successfully defeat the Union and defend themselves, even though some crackpots thought it may be possible. Lincoln's threats were a direct challenge to the courage and the honor of Southern men in a day when honor was so highly prized it led to deadly duels with pistols. However, Lincoln's threat's to their honor was not the most fundamental concern of the South; they feared an invasion and began to prepare to defend themselves and their territory.

Every State had the difficult task of determining if secession would be in their best and wisest self-interest?" No State wanted war and no State had any thought or intention of invading the North before the war began. Looming over all was the Virginia secession convention. The convention was called to decide if Virginia would secede or remain in the Union. On April 4, 1861, "unionist strength in the Virginia convention was such that an ordinance of immediate secession was rejected by a margin of eighty-nine to forty-five." But Lincoln did not know about their vote to remain in the Union when he summoned the Virginia Governor.

Lincoln was exceedingly anxious about Virginia and on Monday, April 1, he authorized Secretary Seward to summon Virginia Governor Sumner to come to Washington. The Governor sent John B. Baldwin to meet with Lincoln. Baldwin arrived late on the morning of April 4th and Lincoln led him to a room that would insure privacy. (Baldwin also did not know about the vote taken in Virginia on that day.) Lincoln asked Baldwin why the unionists had not adjourned the convention yet, and his question bewildered Baldwin. Baldwin assured Lincoln that unionists held a firm majority.

Then Lincoln asked about Fort Sumter. (Lincoln had already made his decision to try to resupply Fort Sumter on March 31st but he did not tell Baldwin) Lincoln was worried about how Fort Sumter would influence the vote in Virginia. Baldwin said: "Sir, it seems to me that our true policy is to hold the position that we have, and for you to uphold our hands by a conservative, conciliatory, national course." Lincoln asked him to explain the course. Baldwin replied that it would include a proclamation of a peace policy without surrendering national authority and withdrawing from Fort Sumter and Pickens. Lincoln said: "What if relief was attempted in a way that could not reasonably be interpreted as aggressive?" "Absolutely not", Baldwin replied. "Confederate forces would never allow it, and any conflict at all would chase the upper South from the Union. If there is a gun fired at Sumter—I don't care on which side it is fired—the opportunity for settlement is lost." He warned Lincoln that in the event of a collision "Virginia, herself, strong as the Union majority in the convention is now, will be out in forty-eight hours." He added that other States hanging in the balance would also be out.

Baldwin did not know, and Lincoln did not tell him, that on March 31st, he had already made the decision to send a fleet of supply ships, accompanied by the Union's most powerful warship, to Fort Sumter. If Lincoln had stayed out of Charleston Harbor, Virginia and other States would have stayed in the Union and the Cotton Belt could have been marginalized. Baldwin's predictions became a reality.

Of course, emotions were strong, but in the first meeting of the Confederate government, sober men prevailed over militant zealots like Robert Rhett and they looked for ways to avoid war. They hoped that no one would act before months of deliberations and negotiations. They hoped that time would become their friend. They appointed a committee of three men to go to Washington and try to negotiate the future of Federal Forts in their territory, including Fort Sumter, but Lincoln refused to meet with them. Let me repeat; they wanted to talk with Lincoln about Fort Sumter before the ships were deployed, but Lincoln would not talk with them. They sent a peace commission to Washington that was also snubbed. They hoped that Washington would listen to their grievances and make an offer to redress them.

Lincoln's offer before the war was to allow the South to keep their slaves. To the South, his offer to let them keep what they already had was frivolous. Their possession of slaves was never an important issue except in the new territories. Lincoln tragically believed that any Southern resistance to the Union army could be quickly and easily smashed and the war would be won quickly with little bloodshed. That was a grave mistake. Lincoln promised war. He said he would go to war if States tried to secede. He kept that promise. He broke his promise to the South that he "would never assail them." It is beyond the realm of reason to think that the seceded States wanted a war.

CHAPTER THREE

SECESSION

E. A. Pollard, editor of the *Daily Richmond Examiner* from 1861 to 1867, wrote: "The two great political schools of America—that of consolidation and that of States' Rights—were founded on different estimates of the relations of the General Government to the States. All other controversies in the political history of the country were subordinate and incidental to this great division of politics." He was right. The controversies began by 1777 and continue until this day. The Constitutional right of a State to secede was raised and argued numerous times before 1861. The most prominent men in the nation made strong cases for both sides of the issue.

Early in his political career, Lincoln argued for a State's Constitutional right to secede. He said: "Any people, anywhere, being inclined and having the power, have the right to rise up and shake off the existing Government, and form a new one that suits them better. Nor is the right confined to cases where the existing Government may choose to exercise it. Any portion of such people that can, may revolutionize, putting down a minority intermingled with, or near about them, who may oppose them." It doesn't much matter now if a constitutional right existed; the issue became moot in 1861. In 1861 the rise of central power and the down spiral of State rights began.

Before the war, the South was a clearly stratified society. Plantation owners were recognized as the upper class. There was a middle class of doctors, lawyers, merchants, businessmen, and black families that owned black slaves in Louisiana and other States. Poor whites and slaves composed the lower class. Class distinctions were clear and generally accepted. The plantation owners became an aristocracy with money, power, and responsibilities. The South was proud of the high value it placed on manners and etiquette. Poor whites were recognized as a class above the black race, even though free blacks in the South owned plantations and slaves and had higher incomes and better living conditions than most poor whites. This was also true of some plantation slaves who learned skills and were given extra ways to earn extra money.

The aristocracy in the South was accepted and respected by practically all white people and free blacks, and nearly all slaves. It was a stable society with defined and accepted class distinctions and without serious class or race conflicts. It was an aristocracy that was working. The local and State governments were elected without serious disruption and they valued their independence. Upward mobility was difficult but there was never a hint of rebellion in the Cotton Belt against the social order. The introduction of industry, machinery, and technology was beginning to change the economy and society in a normal, natural, and gradual way that would have doomed slavery to eventual extinction without the war. But that was not to be. The first and second civil wars brought changes that were abrupt, drastic, and difficult for everyone.

What was the environment in other nations in the 1800s? England feared the expansions of the Union because "the despised colonies of four-score years before had now become a predatory and dangerous empire, filling up the North American continent and threatening, by its existence, the British Empire." (Gore Vidal) By 1861 the nation was brimming over with aggressive expansionist ambitions. What we could not buy, we conquered. We annexed Texas and California by shamelessly going to war with the much weaker Mexico. Lincoln, among others, believed the Mexican war was a disgrace but ambitious leaders made the decisions and to war we went. The nation had a never-satisfied lust for more land. We were still in the noble campaigns of conquering the Indians and confiscating their land. Lincoln enlisted in the Illinois militia to fight "hostile" Indians led by the notorious Black Hawk who had the absurd notion that the land belonged to him and he would not let the paleface have it without a fight. We were building an Empire and, in 1861, a minority of the voters elected a man who would not be satisfied with anything less than being President of all the States and an expanding Empire. He let the plantation owners know they could keep their existing land and slaves but they could not share in the expansion into the new territories—and that he would never allow a State to exit the Union.

The South was frustrated and the economy was sinking before the war. The South rightly believed that a major cause of their declining economy was the unequal legislation of Congress and the constant discrimination of the benefits of the Union between the two sections of the country. Congress established tariffs to protect Northern industries. The tax increased the cost of needed imports for the South and protected Northern factories from foreign competition. A convention of Northern men, excluding Southern representatives, designed and promoted the protective tariff of 1828. Sectional legislation exacted from the South a large portion of the proceeds of Southern industries and gave it to the North in the form of bounties to manufacturers and multiple appropriations. The first tariff was in a temporary war measure in 1818 that lived on and was renewed in 1820, 1824, and increased in 1828. Southern congressmen pled for relief and a compromise was enacted in 1833; that was repudiated in 1842. A system of high duties was also placed on navigation that further protected the North and placed a hardship on Southern commodities.

Southern States were angry about taxation without representation because Northern politicians were in control and paid little attention to the wishes or grievances of the South. Population in the North grew rapidly from the high flow of immigrants attracted to Northern manufacturing and other industries that were booming. For instance, Virginia had ten members to six from New York in the first House of Representative, but in 1860, Virginia had eleven and New York had thirty. South Carolina had only four representatives. The South saw nothing ahead but continued favoritism in Washington for the North and harmful legislation for the South. The direction of change was steadily increasing economic harm for the South by their inclusion in the Union with no realistic hope for a reversal of the direction.

The South's anger was aggravated by insults that came from abolitionists and radicals, but <u>not</u> from ordinary common Northern citizens. Harriet Beecher Stowe's *Uncle Tom's Cabin* became a best seller and a melodrama acted out in theaters throughout the North. Preachers pounced on slavery and made it a righteous cause and painted the South as barbaric. The sermons of Methodist preachers rained hell fire on the monstrous slave holders; <u>but</u>, Northern States had enacted laws prohibiting black people from moving into their States and had enacted Black Codes that enforced segregation in States where there were some black residents. The abolitionists spread pamphlets in Southern towns urging slaves to run away, refuse to work, and create mischief throughout the South. In spite of their loud propaganda, abolitionists remained a small minority in the

North. This is something many people have never known. The trouble was stirred and the war was caused by a radical minority. (Proof of this is documented in other places in the text.)

The South was angry and frightened by the bellicose warnings of Lincoln and Northern radicals. They were frightened by the bloody riots and mass murders on the Kansas border. They were frightened by Mat Turner's attempt to incite a revolution among plantation slaves. They were frightened by the gory murders of white people by the fanatic lunatic John Brown.

John Brown, with his long white beard, ignored his parental responsibilities for his twenty children by two wives to become a self-appointed savior and relentless avenger of slave owners. His raid on Harper's Ferry was simply the culmination of a long trail of "rescues" and bloody atrocities that added fuel to anti-slavery agitation. John Brown's intention, like Nat Turner's, was to incite disobedience and rebellion among Southern slaves. They had little success.

The South believed the Rail-splitter's threats and was alarmed. Southern leaders and common people became genuinely afraid of an invasion and their fears were well grounded. They began to mobilize to defend their land. They wanted Lincoln to know that they could not be intimidated and would resist an invasion. Only a moron could believe that the South wanted a military war with a Union that was stronger in every way. Only a deluded moron could believe that any reasonable person in the South entertained the idea of invading Union territory before the war began. However, some radical northern Republicans and abolitionists itched for a war and were spreading rumors that a Confederate army was planning an attack on Washington.

After the first battle of Bull Run, the Confederate army had an opportunity to attack Washington and invade Union territory. General Jackson told General Lee that he could easily take the city of Washington with 20,000 more troops but General Lee did not want him to invade Washington. Throughout the war Lee, like Generals on both sides, were hoping that Lincoln would agree to a peace settlement and spare the nation from a bloodbath. Lee did not enter Union territory until he went into Maryland and Pennsylvania hoping to pressure Lincoln into accepting an armistice and peace negotiations. He knew that the Confederate forces could not outlast the Union forces in a war of attrition; which it became. He did not anticipate the battle of Gettysburg; he took troops into

Gettysburg primarily to obtain shoes and food for his hungry and shoeless men and thought there would be little resistance.

Before the war, Southern States saw no hope for a redress of their grievances if Lincoln was elected. They genuinely believed that their future would become bleaker in the Union and their hopes could be brighter outside of the Union. Rapid expansion was occurring into the new territories like Texas, Missouri, Kansas, and California and fueled fights within the territories for power and control of the new territories. (Wars are always about power, control, territory, money, and women.) In a hard fought constitutional compromise, a black man was counted as three fifths of a vote and the expansion of plantations and slavery into new territories could eventually give the South (Democrats) an advantage in votes. Radical Republicans would not let that happen. After Lincoln's election, Southern States saw the handwriting on the wall. They knew it was impossible to win anything close to equal representation in Washington. They were naturally feeling frustrated and impotent about their situation in the Union. States seceded for all of the above reasons but they did not secede to preserve the slavery that already existed in their States. Lincoln said many times that he had no intention or <u>desire</u> to interfere with slavery that already existed. He also said it would be unconstitutional. He would not and did not go to war to free the slaves.

People are still deliberately and knowingly, or ignorantly, lying when they insist that the Civil War was fought to free the slaves. Mrs. Goodwin acknowledges that Lincoln wanted and tried hard to convince the nation that the war was for the sole purpose of preserving the Union and not to free the slaves. (The word "sole" means "only.") Lincoln knew that common people in the North would not fight for any other reason. He carefully and deliberately tried to reassure the Northern white population that his partial Presidential Emancipation Proclamation was only a necessary war measure.

Before, and well into the first year of the war, the only measure regarding the slaves that Lincoln proposed (and was still promoting) was colonization. Freedom for slaves was never a serious concern on the President's mind until the war was going badly for the Union and he was mistaken convinced by radicals and Free Blacks that a Presidential Emancipation Proclamation would help the Union's war efforts. Free black leaders and radicals were telling Lincoln that the plantation slaves would rebel and come into Union held territory and fight for the Union if he issued the Proclamation. They were disappointed when he issued the Proclamation and slaves did not flee from the South as they hoped. Fredrick began urging Lincoln to covertly send people into ceded States to try to persuade slaves to leave the plantations. The vast majority of plantation slaves remained in their homes where they had shelter, food, and work. Contrary to common belief and manufactured legends, runaway slaves were very few in number and I will document the fact in 1860 and 1870 census statistics.

Some displacements of slaves did occur when Union troops overran plantations. When plantation owners left, numerous slaves followed Union troops to obtain food because it was the only way they knew of to obtain food. This was their first experience of depending on hand-outs, rather than knowing they earned their livelihood. Legislation of Government grants began immediately after the war. (Abolitionists had highly mistaken ideas about the most typical plantation slaves, just as many people have today.)

Before the war, Lincoln was careful to avoid association with strong abolitionists. His one contact with Frederick Douglas, the foremost free black abolitionists, was to try to convince him, and the delegation of free blacks with him, to promote colonization. Douglas consider it an insult; probably an act of racial bigotry. Freedom for the slaves was distasteful for the mass of Northern common white people before, during, and. even, after the war. (The Union troops were removed from the seceded States in 1877 because, most of all, the Northern population was insisting that they be brought home—much to the chagrin of radical abolitionists and radical Republicans who wanted to continue military rule in those States.)

Slavery was far from a serious sectional problem in 1860, except in the rhetoric of free Black leaders and avid abolitionists. The core of the conflict was about sectional animosity, economics, and political power. The black race became a pawn, more than a cause, of the war. Slavery came into the picture mostly over fights to occupy new territories. Lincoln told Southern plantation owners that they could keep their slaves because slavery was constitutional and he had no legal right, *desire*, or intention of interfering with the institution of slavery in their states—but, in the new territories slavery must be illegal and forbidden—otherwise, Republicans could lose control of Congress and, heaven help them, even the Presidency. The fight then, as now, was between States and the Federal Government. Let me repeat, the war was about money, power, and control. Lincoln and radical

Republicans wanted a strong central government, control of Congress, and control of all of the States. That is an indisputable fact—however much or little you think it was a major cause of the war.

Plantation slavery in the South and factory slaves in Northern States (mostly New York) had never been a serious bone of contention between common people in different sections of the country. Northern abolitionists denigrated Southern slave owners but a large majority of common people in the North could care less about slavery and black people. They just wanted black people to remain in the South. The frank desire of these people was that black people would not move into their States and I cite laws enacted by States before the war. Politicians also wanted to keep slaves out of the new territories for political reasons.

In his first inaugural address Lincoln said: "I have no purpose, directly or indirectly, to interfere with the institution of slavery in the States where it exists. I believe I have no lawful right to do so, and I have no inclination to do so. Those who nominated and elected me did so with full knowledge that I had made this, and many similar declarations, and had never recanted them."

In an election speech Lincoln said: "When they (the South) remind us of their constitutional rights (to own slaves) I acknowledge them, not grudgingly but fully and fairly; and I would give them any legislation for the reclaiming of their fugitives." As I have said, Stephen Douglas, Lincoln's opponent in the election for President, advocated letting each State, including new States, decide for themselves by voting on allowing or forbidding slavery in their State. He also wisely hoped that gradual emancipation could ease some of the social mayhem of an abrupt emancipation and could ameliorate racial integration into a more natural and amicable process. Lincoln and Republicans in congress rejected the proposal to allow States to decide the issue for themselves. (The history of our nation would be entirely different if Douglas, instead of Lincoln, had won the presidential election.)

Lincoln clearly tried hard to prevent the Northern population from believing that freeing the slaves was his reason to go to war. In a message to Horace Greely, Lincoln said: "My paramount object in this struggle is to save the Union and is not to either save or destroy slavery. If I could save the union without freeing any slave I would do it, and if I could save it by freeing all the slaves I would do it; and if I could save it by freeing some slaves and leaving others alone I would also do that. What I do about slavery and the colored race, I do because I believe it will help save the Union and what I forbear, I forbear because I do not believe it will help save the Union." Slavery was never a decisive issue in Lincoln's mind, except slavery in the new territories.

Perhaps there is some psychological need for many in the nation and the black race to hold on to the childish illusion that they had a Champion and a Great Emancipator in Lincoln and that he went to war to free the slaves. Perhaps it is good for the black race to believe that hundreds of thousands of white men from the North went to war and died to end slavery and set them free. That is a con job and hogwash but some historians still believe what they want to believe. They may always refuse to accept the fact that Lincoln really meant what he said.

Lincoln went to war to preserve the Dominion of the Union and he convinced Union troops that was the sole and only purpose of the war. He went to war to force the seceded States to return to the Union. He went to war to preserve the power and domain of one Central Government and to make seceded States submit to Federal control. He won the war and changed America but not for the reason that most people have been taught. Lincoln never intended to be a great emancipator; he was a shrewd man who did what he considered necessary to preserve the Union. (I am providing copious documentation to prove the above assertions.)

We do not know if Lincoln ever seriously entertained a hope that the South would accept his offers of leaving slavery in the South alone and, with this reassurance, return to the Union. The South fought because they had been invaded. A huge majority of white people in the South were not slave owners and could not have wanted war to keep slaves they never had.

Of the 6,184,477 people in the Slave States in 1860, only 347,525 were plantation and slave owners. In 1860 there was a population of 18,647 free black people living in Louisiana and a significant number of those free black people owned slaves. The total number of black and white residents in Louisiana was almost equal. (New York had a population of 49,005 black residents in 1860; Illinois had 7,628; and Pennsylvania had 56,849 black people in their total population of 2,906,115. Other Northern States had no, or very few, black residents.) The census also stated that, during the census period of 1850 to 1860, a total of 803 slaves ran away; or about one in 5,000. Historians would have us believe that thousands of slaves were running away. Many more slaves were voluntarily set free than ran away. Twenty thousand slaves were freed by their owners in the decade of 1950 to 1960.

By the time Lincoln became President, the Southern States wanted independence and sovereignty for their States and wanted freedom to leave the Union. The prevailing sentiment of the majority in the North was that they did not want black people, free or slave, to live among them and the overwhelming majority of white people would never have waged war if they thought it was to free the slaves. Proof of this statement is abundant. Most Northern common people did not give a damn about black people.

Here is a sampling of quotes from Northern newspapers: "It is neither for the good of the colored race nor of our own that they should (Sic) continue to dwell among us to any extent. The two races can never exist in conjunction except as superior and inferior . . . The African is naturally the inferior race. (*Philadelphia Daily News*, November 22, 1860) This is a Northern newspaper.

"Evil and nothing but evil, has ever followed in the track of this hideous monster, Abolition. Let (the slave) alone—send him back to his master where he belongs." (*Chicago Daily Times*, December 7, 1860. This is another Northern newspaper.

"The immense increase in the number (of slaves) within so short a time speaks for the good treatment and happy, contented lot of the slaves. They are comfortable, fed, housed and clothed, and seldom or never overworked." (*New York Herald*, March 7, 1861). This was a common sentiment in Northern newspapers.

"The proposition that the Negro is equal by nature, physically and mentally, to the white man, seems to be so absurd and preposterous, that we cannot conceive how it can be entertained by any intelligent and rational white man." (*Concord Democrat Standard*, September 8, 1860)

In January, 1850, Henry Clay, regarded by Lincoln as an ideal statesman, introduced an ominous bill that clearly set boundaries and named the States and Territories in which slave possession would and would not be permitted. He warned that only by compromise, by give and take, by each side North and South making concessions could the Union be saved. He rebuked the personal ambitions of people using the controversy about slavery in new territories to gain political power. Daniel Webster spoke in favor of the bill and it passed and became law. The passage was celebrated by processions, bonfires, booming cannons and speeches. A period of calm settled in over the country. "In many a house men breathed easier and slept better because secession and possibly war had been stood off. The quiet was broken only by the abolitionists, Free-Soilers, and antislavery men flinging insults and stirring passions of self-righteousness."

Two years later, 1852, (eight years before Lincoln became a candidate for President) Lincoln said: "The nation has passed its perils, and is free, prosperous, and powerful." Douglas said there was no reason why the nation could not remain half-slave and half-free as it had for many years since its founding. The institution of slavery was already beginning to wane and was doomed to eventual extinction by natural economic and cultural evolutionary dynamics in play. Douglas was talking, in part, about the impact of changes already taking place in slavery by the rapidly increasing number of mulattoes and changing economics. In 1852 there were 3,204,000 slaves in the nation. In 1850, there were 348,874 mulattoes in the South and 56,649 mulattoes in the North. Black people and white people were becoming brown people. Most mulattoes in the North were not born in the North but had immigrated from the South. The number of free Negroes who became slave holders was rising. However, the economic value of slave labor was beginning to disappear.

The peace that prevailed after the Missouri Compromise was broken by the Supreme Court giving itself exalted and unconstitutional power in the Dred Scott case; the nefarious unconstitutional assumption of the power to review an act of Congress. The Court declared the Missouri Compromise unconstitutional. Angry contention rose again and destroyed the peace that the compromise made possible—and may have made the secession of States and the first civil war inevitable. (Chief Justice Taney, who read the Dred Scott decision, had once inherited some slaves but he set all of them free except for three who were too old to work, and he let them remain so that he could care for them. He was not an evil man and did not hate black people. But his court trashed the Constitution.)

Why do I call the exercise of power by the Supreme Court to review an act of Congress unconstitutional? (I will now, and later, use the research and writings of a brilliant genuine statesman, Gore Vidal, for facts and information.)

The Supreme Court actually preceded Lincoln in abrogating the Constitution's checks and balances. There are now essentially no checks on the Supreme Court's desire to expand its powers. The Constitution clearly gives Congress the power to regulate the Court—and not the other way around. Article III of the Constitution clearly states: "The Supreme Court shall have appellate jurisdiction, both as to law and fact, with such exceptions and <u>under such regulations as the Congress</u> shall make. Let me repeat: The Constitution clearly states that Congress shall regulate the appellate jurisdiction of the Supreme Court and place exceptions on its appellate powers. It does not say that the Supreme Court can regulate Congress and nullify acts of Congress. The President can do that with the power of his veto and the people can vote a Congressman out of office.

The Supreme Court and Presidential "Fiats" have effectively excised the gonads of Congress and exalted their own powers. The decisions of the expanded powers of the Supreme Court have actually had both good and bad results; but that is not the problem. The Supreme Court now holds the strongest seat of power in our nation. They now constitute the premier authority and most powerful branch of the government; but the President is not far behind. This development is welcomed by people who want control of individual States by the Central Government. The Civil War erupted when States believed that the only way they could hold on to their authority, rights, and control was to secede.

Lincoln had the power in his hands to back, bolster, and employ the wisdom of the Missouri Compromise in his decisions; but he chose not to. Instead he aggravated and agitated tension with passionate speeches against secession and the right of States to determine by popular vote the question of slavery in the new territories. He and the Federal Government wanted the power to make that decision in Washington. Here is the core of the principal conflict and cause of the war. I repeat; it was about power, control, and the secession of States. He said: "My enemies now say that I am carrying on the war for the sole purpose of abolition. It is, and will be carried on as long as I am President for the sole purpose of restoring the Union." The definition of the word "sole" is: "Being the only one; existing or functioning without another." Sole purpose means it was the only purpose that was crucially important to Lincoln.

Hinton R. Helper published *The Impending Crisis of the South* citing evolving statistics. "As a general rule, poor white persons are regarded with less esteem and attention than Negroes and though the condition of the latter is wretched . . . . vast numbers of the former are infinitely worse off." Edwin A. Pollard wrote about a different kind of slavery in the North. "Our (Southern) slaves are hired for life and well compensated. Yours are

29

hired by the day, not cared for and scantily compensated . . . . Why you meet more beggars in the city of New York than you would meet in a lifetime in the whole South . . . . Your slaves are white, of your own race . . . If they knew that the ballot box is stronger than an army of bayonets, and could combine (form unions), where would you be? Your society would be reconstructed, your government overthrown, your property divided." His prescience was uncanny.

Another historian described the situation in the North like this: "For the Northern man, abolition was at first a hateful idea. He had no use for the black man as slave—but did not want him as a neighbor either." When the second election for president was looking dire for Lincoln, and friends were telling him that it was impossible for him to be elected again, Lincoln replied that many in the North were <u>mistakenly</u> believing that the war was being fought to free the slaves and that was the reason so many were turning against him. Di Lorenzo said that (before the war began): "There was indeed a vigorous abolitionist movement in parts of the North, but it was a small movement; so small that politicians like Lincoln did not risk associating themselves with it. The overwhelming majority of white people treated the blacks who lived among them with contempt, ridicule, discrimination, and sometimes violence."

After touring America to learn what the cultures and conditions of people all over the country were like, the renowned Frenchman, Alex de Tocqueville, said: "The prejudice of race appears to be stronger in the states that have abolished slavery than in those where it still exists; and nowhere is it so intolerant as in those states where servitude has never been known." In *North of Slavery*, Eugene Berwanger said: "In virtually every phase of existence (in the North) Negroes found themselves systematically segregated from whites . . . they could not enter most hotels, restaurants, and resorts, except as servants; they prayed in "Negro pews" in the white churches and if partaking of the sacrament they waited until the whites had been served the bread and wine. Moreover, they were often educated in segregated schools; punished in segregated prisons; nursed in segregated hospitals; and buried in segregated cemeteries . . . racial prejudice haunts its victim wherever he goes." In 1853, Sarah Parker Remond, a freeborn black abolitionist, purchased a ticket for an opera performance at Boston's Howard Athenaeum. The theater manager not only refused to seat her but had her thrown out injuring her in the process.

In 1827, John Marvin, a free black man, went to Ohio to establish a home and wrote: "I thought upon coming to a free state like Ohio that I would find every door open to receive me, but from the treatment I received by the people generally, I found it little better than in Virginia . . . . I found every door closed against the colored man in a Free State, except the jails."

In 1837, the free black leader Frederick Douglass wrote: "There is not perhaps . . . a city in which prejudice against color is more widespread than in Philadelphia . . . Colored persons, no matter how well dressed or well behaved, are not even permitted to ride on any of the many railways through that Christian city."

Lincoln prosecuted a war that was fomented by the rich or powerful radicals that always pose the gravest danger to peace within any nation. It was never a democratic decision of the majority or the will of common people in the North or the South to fight the bloody war. After Fort Sumter, Lincoln had to find a way to raise war passions and a willingness in the North to fight in a war that only a minority fostered. (The majority is not always right and, perhaps, in this case Lincoln was right and the majority was wrong. How can we ever know?) Lincoln confessed that he was driven by overpowering ambition, but, I am sure that he would much rather have been able to accomplish his goal without a war—but when he issued loud bellicose warnings during his campaign speeches, he put himself in a box.

Now Lincoln faced Fort Sumter. He could have waited for peaceful negotiations to try to resolve the conflicts but he was pressured and chose war. For decades, Hamilton fought for a strong Central Government and Jefferson fought for independence and self-determination for the States. The Civil War decided the issue. The war was fought; the Union, Lincoln, and Hamilton won. It was one of the most decisive points in our history and the genesis of our powerful Federal Government. Since the power and domain of our Central Government was firmly established, it has continued on a zigzag rise toward Imperialistic powers in Washington D. C. When the chips were down, Lincoln resorted to using force to preserve the Union. Reputable historians and statesmen are now making strong arguments that, with time and other methods, slavery could have been eliminated and the Union saved without the bloody war.

I believe the South has been misrepresented as the blackest villain and that they fought only for ignoble reasons. My grandmother's generation is painted as heinous. Biased historians cast a dark blinding cloud over truth, factual information, and an honest helpful understanding of our history and people, as they really were and really are. I hate any patronizing attitude toward the black race and poor white people. I hate the insulting lies that I read in books and hear on television; lies that perpetuate prejudice and pour acid on sectional and political tensions and exacerbate virulent racism. Here is one example that was published in 2010.

In my opinion, one of the most biased, insulting, shallow, incorrect, and just plain dumb books written about the South and the Confederate soldiers that I have read is *The Long Shadow of the Civil War.* It was written by Victoria Bynum, professor of history at Texas States University. In my opinion, she has sarcasm and slander drooling from her mouth when she talks about the old South—except when she paints certain Southern Confederate army deserters as heroes and their wives as heroines. I believe that she was snickering and sarcastically mocking what she refers to as the "lost cause" of the civil war. She writes about Confederate soldiers that deserted and, while they were hiding, looted and killed white people. She seems to want to transform them into champions of opposition to the bad South. The deserters are the good guys and the Confederate troops that try to capture them are the bad guys.

Ms. Bynum, Confederate deserters were captured and shot or hanged in the South just like Union deserters in the North—but I found no mention of the capture and execution of Union deserters. She emphasizes opposition to the war by Southern people. Of course, the South was not "solid" in wanting and supporting the war but neither was the North. An immense majority of common people in the North and South did not want the war.

Ms. Bynum does not mention the riot in New York against conscription and the Presidential Emancipation Proclamation. In July, 1863, there was a violent race riot in New York protesting the partial Emancipation Proclamation and conscription demands. Mobs of white men roamed the streets of New York for days. They attacked police, Republican abolitionists, and Blacks. They set fire to an orphanage for black children. They attacked and killed black men and boys in the downtown tenement district and any black person unfortunate enough to be found in the streets. They hanged William Jones (a black man) and set his body on fire. They set fire to the building that housed the *New York Tribune.* All shops were shut and all carriages and omnibuses stopped running. Telegraph wires were cut and railroad tracks torn up. The riots were not quelled until Lincoln sent five regiments of Federal troops to New York. The troops gained the upper hand and stopped the rioting by shooting and killing between 300 and 1000 citizens—no one knows the exact number of deaths.

On August 4, 1862, Lincoln issued a second call for 300,000 troops. Historian Carl Sandburg wrote: "Men who did not want to go to war, by thousands, filed exemption claims . . . In ten days, 14,000 claims were filed in New York City. Thousands were crossing into Canada or buying steamship tickets to Europe . . . Resistance and evasion of the attempts of the state government spread so far that the President issued a proclamation that 'all persons discouraging volunteer enlistments, resisting militia drafts, or guilty of any disloyal practice' would come under martial law—and the writ of habeas corpus would be useless in any jail where they were held."

Resistance to the war in the North was broader and more vehement than it was in the South. When the war became a long, hard, blood bath and the Confederates were winning battle after battle during the first two years, Lincoln became frustrated, hardened, and enraged. He was disappointed and angry at his generals, deserting Union soldiers, and the angry opposition to the war in the North. Deserters were shot or hanged in both the North and South. You may not know that on December 26, 1862, in Mankato, Minnesota, one of the largest mass executions of army deserters in US history was carried out. (Washington Post: Five Myths about Lincoln.)

In my opinion, Ms. Bynum demeans and mocks the motivation of Confederate troops to fight in their (snicker, snicker) "lost cause." That includes my step grandfather. God, I detest that woman. Since the majority of common people in both the North and the South did not want the war before it began, both sides had to use conscription. However, both Union and Confederate soldiers fought bravely and heroically on bloody battlefields and all of them deserve honor and respect much more than sarcastic denigration; which Ms. Bynum seems to heap primarily on the South. I believe that she, like many other historians, is a politically correct propagandist, myth maker, and promoter of prejudice toward the South. I believe her animus is blatant.

This morning, September 26, 2011, there were some back and forth comments between people on the internet about the Confederate flag. They identify themselves only by their first name. Here is one from Will that is fairly typical: "The Confederate flag is as much a symbol of hate and racism as the Nazi flag is. It represents a government that went to war to defend its ability to enslave human beings . . . Yes, the Confederate flag is a symbol of the Southern heritage and culture, but unfortunately that is not exactly something to be proud of."

Dale said: "The civil war was caused by the manipulation of southern press by a relatively few wealthy slave/land owners. They initiated a fear and hate campaign which incited treason . . . The Confederate battle flag represents treason and oppression."

I hope that this prejudice and denigration of the South on the internet is not the common thinking of most people in our nation. The Confederate flag deserves honor and respect as a symbol of the courageous fight of Confederate soldiers to defend their land, their honor, and their independence. The Confederate flag has been misused by stupid people in the 20th century like bikers and skinheads and other deranged people but that is not the fault of the flag and is not a valid reason for anyone to spit on the flag. Wrongly and sadly, the flag has been perverted from a symbol of men fighting bravely for their home into a politically correct symbol of shame and racism.

It is a fact that racism was rampant in the South just as it was in the North, but if we condemn the Confederate flag as a symbol of racism, then the American flag should also be condemned as a symbol of nation-wide racism; racism that was terribly exacerbated by our first and second civil wars. Racism is not as open and patent now as it was in the 1800s but it is still an ugly blight on the whole nation and has shameful consequences. It was wrong and unjust to brand white Southerners and the Confederate troops as criminals—and to treat them like criminals when the war was over. Lincoln did not want it to be like that. The South has been maligned and I am defending my dear old Dixie and attacking sectional and racial prejudices wherever I see them.

Hopefully, we will never again fight an awful military war between sections of the country. Sectional and political party conflicts plunged us into our civil war. The major blame for the war has been unfairly placed on the South. Unless we are the United States of Amnesia, as Gore Vidal asserts, we can learn valuable lessons from our history, if we know our history and the history is accurate; and we are wise So, I pick up my trusty musket, load it, and fire away.

Today, the most and worst prejudice and racism is not in the South; it is in the large cities all over the country that have become traps and incubators of black poverty and understandable valid anger and discontent. One reason why prejudice and racism are intractable is because they are used as tools of politicians fighting for more and more power and control, just as it was before, during, and after the civil war. I firmly believe that the South now plays the race card in politics less than any other section of the country. My home town of Pineville, Louisiana, with a population that is 85% white, recently elected a black mayor and then reelected him without opposition. The people love him. He was elected on his merit; not his color. We still have problems of prejudice and racism in the South but not as bad as the cities of New York, Chicago, and Los Angeles. Now take that, Chris and Bill.

CHAPTER FOUR

THE DECISION

On March 31, 1861, Lincoln made a decision that changed the world. His decision determined the shape and size of our nation and the kind of government we would have. It probably affected the kind of wars our nation was involved in after his death. It affected the kind of people we are. It molded history and without the war, perhaps, someone else, rather than you and I might be alive today; I guess that should make me thankful. The history shaping decision on March 31st was Lincoln's decision to try to resupply Fort Sumter. He was probably already angry at South Carolina because they were the first State to secede. Lincoln had been vigorously warned that South Carolina would not allow Federal ships and troops to enter Charleston harbor. The decision to resupply Fort Sumter caused more States to secede and Lincoln carried out his threats and used Fort Sumter as justification for invading Confederate territory.

Most radical Republicans did not want to evacuate Fort Sumter because they thought it would be a capitulation to rebellion that would destroy the country; some Democrats urged evacuation because they thought nothing was more certain to destroy the country than civil war. Secretary of State and right hand man of Lincoln, William Seward, forcefully argued against trying to resupply Sumter. The top military officer, General Winfred Scott, argued against resupplying and told Lincoln that any attempt at the time was a military impossibility. He cited a large number of troops that would be necessary to successfully invade Confederate territory. Seward tried to reason with Lincoln and told him exactly what would happen if he tried to resupply Fort Sumter. He told Lincoln that it would inevitably provoke the remaining slave States to secede and launch a civil war—that "most disastrous and deplorable of human calamities." Seward was right.

Seward must have thought Lincoln agreed with him and was certain that he would not make the wrong decision and ignite a civil war because he sent a commission to the Confederate Government to tell them that no attempt would be made to resupply the Fort. (Lincoln did not know what Seward had done.) Seward was confident that Lincoln would not try to resupply Sumter. Historian Benjamin Thomas wrote: "Adhering to his policy of appeasement and convinced that Lincoln would adopt his views, Seward assured Campbell in mid-March, that Sumter would be evacuated and pleaded for Southern forbearance, several times repeated, for a pledge. Later both the seceded States and those of the upper South would believe the President guilty of bad faith."

Republicans were concerned about losing a source of income. They had enacted an import tax that was soon doubled and was about to take effect. New Orleans was one of the busiest ports. New York was worried that more imports would come through New Orleans than New York because a seceded State could lower the tax placed on imports. New York officials pressured Lincoln to resupply. Stress became severe when Lincoln delayed his decision and the radicals lambasted him for his "inactivity." Radical firebrands like Montgomery Blair brought relentless pressure on Lincoln and questioned why he was waiting. The *New York Times* scolded Lincoln in an editorial for vacillating and his "indecision."

Lincoln polled his cabinet on March 15 and five were opposed to supplying Fort Sumter; one was undecided, and one was in favor. Days later, after gathering additional information, he polled his cabinet again and three were for and three were against. William Howard Russell, of the *London Times,* talked to Ambassador George Bancroft who said: "as a Government it had no power to coerce the people of the South or to save itself from danger." At a dinner of top New York Democrats, everyone present agreed that the Government did not have the right to force a State to remain in the Union. All but one New York democratic newspaper wrote that a military solution would be more destructive than peaceful secession. The Northern Democrats enjoyed watching Republicans squirm. After all, the whole thing was about politics.

I believe that Lincoln's decision to light the fuse and go to war may have been the worst decision any United States President has ever made.

Lincoln naturally, wanted to make the South appear as the aggressors; the side that started the war. Lincoln made Fort Sumter his *casus belli.* Fort Sumter became his "remember the Alamo"; "remember the Maine"; "remember Tonkin Bay." The twist given to the story of Fort Sumter by Lincoln idolizers makes the South the war's aggressors and makes Fort

Sumter the cause of the war. The South fired the first shot against an intrusion into their waters. They had given Lincoln fair warning that they would not allow Union forces to enter Charleston Harbor. They also fired the first shot because they had intercepted a message that Lincoln had dispatched a fleet of ships, including a warship, to Fort Sumter and they wanted to prevent a battle with Union guns in Charleston Harbor by taking Fort Sumter before the Union fleet arrived. Lincoln defied the Confederate warnings. The Confederates saw the approach of unwanted ships in their harbor as a threat, an unacceptable intrusion into Confederate territory, and a provocation. Lincoln tried to employ force, as he said he would, and the Confederates did what they said they would do.

Of course, Lincoln wanted public opinion to make the South guilty of starting the war and lying elite historians agree with him. They have convinced many, perhaps most, people in the nation today that Fort Sumter started and caused the war. They have brain washed many people. The South would never have taking any other military action or try to invade Union territory after the shelling of Fort Sumter. They did not want a war but they were deathly afraid of being invaded and did not want to be intimated or let Lincoln believe they would not fight if invaded. Lincoln had declared war on the South and it began when he invaded Virginia and the first real battle of the war was fought at Bull Run.

Jefferson Davis and Southern Congressmen would have been stupid to want a war; and they were not stupid. They knew that the North had a huge advantage in numbers and resources and did not want, especially, a war of attrition. They would have been worse than stupid to invade Union territory and launch a war. Rational men could never start a war if they knew that they faced a vastly superior opponent. The only advantage that the Confederates had was the energy and resolve granted to all social creatures that are fighting on and defending their own territory. The Confederates strongest desire at that time was to be left alone but they would not surrender without a fight. This was the message that the Confederates sent to Lincoln at Fort Sumter. They were telling him that they would not be cowed and would fight if invaded. Lincoln used it as a rallying cry and began mobilizing and making preparations for war.

We know the story of Fort Sumter and we know historians slant it differently. Fort Sumter, off the coast of Charleston, was running out of supplies and the Union soldiers faced surrender or starvation if they did not receive new supplies from the Federal Government. The

Confederate Commander in Charleston, General Beauregard, asked (and later demanded) the Fort Commander, Major Anderson, to evacuate the Fort and take his soldiers back to Washington—and warned the Union that they would not allow the Fort to be resupplied. Lincoln knew that without new supplies the fort would fall into Confederate hands. (All other Federal Forts in Confederate territory were already under Confederate control; except Fort Pickens at Pensacola.) President Buchanan made a previous attempt to supply the Fort but his ships turned back when the Confederate canons fired warning volleys and nothing more happened. Buchanan did not believe possession of the Fort was worth invading a Southern State and risking a war. Confederate officers intercepted a wire ordering ships to Fort Sumter and believed that Lincoln had lied to hide an invasion. Historian Thomas said that Lincoln was being careful in his deliberations and plans not because he wanted to avoid action but he was "avoiding mistakes."

We should not be surprised by Lincoln's decision to send supply and war ships. He had announced his intentions and was backing his word. When Lincoln gave orders for the ships to proceed to Fort Sumter, he also ordered ships to sail to Pensacola and resupply Fort Pickens. The orders were confused but it made no difference. Confederate canons did exactly what Secretary Seward said they would do before the ships arrived.

On April 12, 1861, the shelling began and continued until the soldiers in Fort Sumter surrendered. The Fort was destroyed. One man was killed during the shelling and that was by an accidental explosion of gunpowder within the fort. The Union soldiers surrendered; were treated with respect and dignity and put on a ship to return home. Lincoln immediately began propaganda to justify war. He called the attack "unprovoked". He and historians made Fort Sumter the cause of the war. Lincoln wanted the world to believe that the South was the aggressor and historians have repeated the lie many times.

None of what I write is intended to make Jefferson Davis and the seceded States faultless or that they carried no responsibility for the war, but the actual fighting did not begin with the shelling of Fort Sumter; it began with the first battle of Bull Run after Union forces invaded Virginia. That battle began eight months after Fort Sumter's surrender. Only a devious interpretation of the facts can make the Confederacy the aggressor and the Union the defender. The first battle began when Confederate territory was invaded. (The first casualties were in Baltimore when a train load of Union troops tried to disembark on one train to board another train. Baltimore citizens were enraged and a riot broke out and some people were killed but that was far from a battle or a launching of the war.)

Who wanted the war? Who was to blame for the war? To me, one of the most disappointing things about Lincoln was that he was bluntly dishonest after the war began; especially in trying to shirk responsibility and playing the "blame game." Perhaps propaganda is a necessary tool in war, but it is still ugly and dishonest. Only a perverse twisting of logic and facts can conclude that the South wanted to start and fight a military war. The South would gladly forego a war if they were allowed to secede. To cite the shelling of Fort Sumter as the cause of the Civil War is nothing less than simplistic stupidity. Let me repeat; it is simplistic stupidity. The reason was that Lincoln said he would use force before he was elected President and he did what he said he would do; he began the war with an invasion after he became President and States seceded. Confederates would not yield and Lincoln would not relent. Neither side was guiltless.

The first real battle of the war began near Manassas, Virginia. Confederate and Union forces gathered and took positions to fight the battle, know as Bull Run. It was on Virginia soil close to Washington. (I visited the initial battlefield and was startled by the smallness of the field and the closeness of the two sides when they began firing.)

Droves of civilian men and women gathered on a hillside, like spectators at a football game, to watch the fighting. Like Lincoln, they were expecting an easy Union victory. Before the day was over, the Confederate army had thoroughly trounced the Union forces and the battle turned into a route with Union soldiers and spectators running for their lives. That is when General William "Stonewall" Jackson told General Robert E. Lee that, if he would give him 20,000 more men, he could easily take the city of Washington. Lee decided against the action. Let me repeat; I believe that both Confederate and Union Generals were still hoping the issues could be settled without mass slaughter.

During the first two years of the war, the South won every major battle and Lincoln became incensed by the failure of Union Generals, like McClellan, to be more aggressive and launch major offensive action against Confederate troops. Antiwar sentiment became overwhelming in the North when Union troops were being defeated and suffering thousands of casualties. Lincoln faced certain defeat in his bid for reelection but he was saved when the tide of war changed.

Each year of the war the South dwindled in the number of their troops and their resources while the North gained. The Northern civilian population was increasing and become wealthier.

Alex de Tocqueville said: "In steel, oil, railroads, munitions, textiles and other industries, scores of large fortunes were made. The fast and luxurious living in most of the Union cities still contrasted with sacrifices on the march, in camp, and battlefields. Travelers from Europe commented in surprise at seeing seaboard cities of a North at war with so few signs of war and such throngs of spenders and pleasure hunters as in no European cities." After the war, the North had a more numerous population, including men, and, except for their debt, was more prosperous than it was before the war. There were 145,551 more voters at the polls (all men) in November '64 in the North than before the war (due largely to immigration). Lincoln said in December: "We have more men now than when the war began, we are not exhausted or in the process of exhaustion, we are gaining strength and may, (sic) if need be, maintain the contest indefinitely." The sacrifices in the North for the Union were in the number of men killed and wounded. That alone is too much sacrifice.

Lee took his Army into Gettysburg primarily to get food and shoes for his soldiers. His men were out of food and many were barefooted. He did not anticipate the battle at Gettysburg. Lee also hoped that he could arouse enough antiwar emotions in the North to make Lincoln sue for peace. He hoped that, by going into Union territory, the Northern people would shout louder for peace. Going into Gettysburg was a tragic mistake for the Confederate forces. If Lee stayed within Confederate boundaries, he could have held out longer and time may have become his friend rather than his enemy.

The sacrifices in the South were not limited to the men killed in battle. Sherman wanted to wage a war against Southern civilians and, even though senior Unions Officers advised against it, Lincoln gave his approval and Sherman began his devastating march of destruction against civilians and the infrastructure. Sherman's war against civilians inflicted devastation on more buildings, homes, cities, infrastructure, food supplies, livestock, and property, than any flood, hurricane, earthquake, or other natural disaster in recorded history. The destruction of civilian property was almost entirely in the South. Starvation became a grim reality. (Sherman did not kill civilians but he killed or took every other living creature.) Sherman tried to convince Lincoln that his tactics could shorten and end the war with fewer casualties; and he was probably right. Lincoln continued a war of attrition.

My maternal grandmother witnessed the horror and suffered like other Southern women and children. That is why she hated Lincoln. Eventually, the South kneeled and surrendered. This was not enough for radical Republican congressmen. Against the wishes and best efforts of Lincoln (I wish my grandmother could have known about that), they insisted on militia law that guaranteed Republican control. They humiliated the South. They wanted the South punished and treated like criminals; and it was.

"Why don't we drop it Jerry? Your friendship means too much to me for us to keep debating the civil war." That is what I said to the retired pastor of the prestigious First Methodist Church of Colorado Springs, Colorado. Jerry and I take an active part in a weekly two hour discussion group called the Philosophical Café. He espouses the conventional narrative about Fort Sumter and the war. In the previous session, Jerry handed me a six page article he clipped out of a recent issue of a magazine about the American Civil War. It was written by Stephanie McCurry.

In my opinion, Ms. McCurry stays true blue to the politically correct version of Lincoln and the war but gives a different and moronic twist to a reason why the South lost the war. Worst of all, she joins others who stir the pot of ill feelings toward the South and the controversy that boiled over in the war between States and the Central Government. She is now another purveyor of another myth.

Ms. McCurry, as I saw her, exposed shades of radical feminism. Her animus is, apparently, toward Southern men. She was right in emphasizing the importance of manly honor in the war but pictured men's concern for honor as nothing more than dumb male macho behavior. She had some correct facts but her assumptions were stupid. She made a clumsy effort to prove her thesis that Southern women opposed the war and tried to undermine Confederate forces and was a reason why the South lost the war. Bravo for women, even Southern women, she implies. Of course, there were men and women in the South, and in the North, who opposed the war, but the vast majority of Southern women did all that they could to support their sons and husbands after the fighting began; and their men were dying. Ms. McCurry's presumptions were created out of silly imaginations. I wish she could have talked to my Grandmother before writing her diatribe. All that I have written about Ms. McCurry are my opinion.

Jean Berlin had pages from a Confederate nurse's diary published. She said: "Ada Bacot's diary is a significant document that can help students, teachers, scholars, and general readers alike understand the role loyal Southern women like Ada Bacot played in the Civil War. The contribution Bacot and other women made to the Confederacy war effort, both directly through nursing and indirectly through ladies' aid associations, fund raising drives, and personal sacrifices, had an immeasurable impact on the South's ability to keep fighting long after its resources ran short."

Ms. McCurry could have found copious documented proof of the aid and support that Southern women provided for soldiers and the war by reading Bell Irvin Wiley's *Confederate Women*. There were some bread riots when women and children were near starvation but that was exceptional and not the characteristic behavior of Confederate women.

Southern women were as angry as the men before the war about the behavior of Lincoln and radical Republican, and the denigration of Southern people in pamphlets and some Northern newspapers. They were angry most of all about the threat to their freedom and independence. The rampage of killing white people by the lunatic abolitionists, John Brown, incensed and frightened them as did the killing in Nebraska and Kansas.

Ms. McCurry exposes her prejudice by making the South the blackest villain and holding fast to the lie that freeing plantation slaves was the primary purpose of the war. She must actually believe that Union soldiers were fighting for that purpose. She succeeds only in throwing more coals on the fire of racism and prejudice—a fire that needs to be extinguished to help correct major problems in the US. There is enough blame for the war to go around to everyone involved but the guilt and innocence of different people and sections of the country have been unevenly assigned by historians who dare not cast aspersions on Lincoln or the conquering Union. The valid intentions of the Confederacy, including self defense, have been impugned since the beginning and end of the actual fighting in the civil war.

The most fundamental grievances in Southern States were, in their consideration, an overreaching and power hungry big Central Government that was injuring them. Russell McClintock said: "Secession was not inherently violent. In actuality, the Civil War began not when the Southern States seceded but when Northern States acted forcibly to stop them. In the end it was Northerners who decided whether it was to be peace or sword." When, after long delays, Lincoln finally succeeded in badgering his Generals into invading Virginia and removed all questions about which side was the aggressor.

CHAPTER FIVE

ENEMY IN THE REAR

During the first two years of the war the Northern armies were badly beaten in all major battles. Lincoln became furious at his Generals, especially McClellan. He called again and again for a massive invasion of Confederate territory. When the Union Army won their first battle it was not enough for Lincoln. He fumed because his Generals did not pursue the retreating Confederate army and annihilate them when they had an advantage. I would like to think that McClellan and other Generals did not relish the prospect of the mass killings and still hoped the sectional quarrel could be settled by cooler heads without a river of blood. It became a war that would be decided by killing and the depletion of Confederate resources and soldiers. Many civilians died of hunger, disease, and starvation in the South. Sentiment in the Northern population against the war grew stronger and stronger as the war proceeded and created a major problem that Lincoln referred to as an "enemy in the rear".

Before Sumter, powerful voices in the North pled with Lincoln to leave the South alone and let them leave. Here is a sampling of the antiwar sentiment of a majority of ordinary citizens in the North. The influential newspaper, the *New York Times,* said on March 21st: "It cannot be denied that there are growing sentiments throughout the North in favor of letting the Gulf States go." (sic) The *Daily National Intelligence* pled with Lincoln to: "Let the South have its experiment in independence." The *Illinois State Journal* said: "The sooner we cut loose from the disaffected States the better it may be for all parties and for the nation." A pro-union paper said: "The south ought to go in peace if it cannot be held by persuasion." The *Delaware Gazette* was in favor of: "Outright diplomatic recognition of the Confederacy."

After the first battle of Bull Run, Horace Greely (Go west young man), the editor of the New York Tribune and one of the most eloquent and influential speakers in the nation, wrote a letter to Lincoln that said: "The gloom in this city is funeral; for our dead at Bull Run were many and they lie unburied yet. On every brow sits sullen, scorching, black despair." He closed the letter with "Yours in the depth of despair." Greely pled with Lincoln for an armistice, a national convention, peace, and disbanding the forces. Lincoln never answered the letter. Nowhere could I find that Lincoln ever considered peace or a negotiated settlement. Lincoln insisted on waging unrelenting war until the Confederacy was decisively defeated and he could enforce obeisance to the Union by every State.

In the summer of 1964, Lincoln called for 500,000 more men to be drafted for the war. The quota for Chicago was 6,000. A mass meeting in Chicago appointed a committee to go to Washington and ask the Secretary of War, Edwin M. Stanton, to lower their enrollment figure. Joseph Medill, editor of the Chicago *Tribune*, was the leader and spokesman for the committee. When Stanton refused their request they went to Lincoln and he agreed to meet with them and Stanton and hear both sides. Lincoln sat quietly and listened as Medill said Chicago had already sent 22,000 men and had no more to send.

When Medill finished his argument, Lincoln lifted his head and this is how Medill reported his reply: "Gentlemen, after Boston, Chicago has (sic) been the chief instrument in bringing this war on the country. The Northwest has opposed the South as the Northeast has opposed the South. You *called for war* until we had it. You called for emancipation and *I have given it to you*. Whatever you have asked for you have (sic) had. Now you come here begging to be let off from the call for men which I have made to carry out the war which you have demanded. You ought to be ashamed of yourselves. I have a right to expect better things of you. Go home and raise your extra 6000 men. And you, Medill, are acting like a coward. You and your *Tribune* have had more influence than any paper in the Northwest in making this war. You can influence great masses and yet you cry to be spared at a moment when your cause is suffering. Go home and send us those men." Medill went home and raised the men.

Newspapers, radical politicians, business men, and abolitionists pressured Lincoln into starting the war. He told them they wanted the war and now they had it. Perhaps many were, at this stage of the war, ready for peace negotiations but Lincoln would not be satisfied until all of the Confederate army was annihilated or surrendered. Pleas for peace commissions from the North and South were repeated but rejected.

Abolitionists and some Congressmen had a sorely mistaken belief that an Emancipation Proclamation would increase the Union soldier's motivation to fight and could incite an up-rising of slaves in the South. They pressured Lincoln to issue his partial Presidential Emancipation Proclamation. This shows us how much the radical leaders were out of touch with common people in the North and slaves in the South. Lincoln was reluctant to issue the Proclamation for a number of reasons. He knew and admitted that it was unconstitutional but he was primarily reluctant because he was afraid that it would not have the desired effect; and, I hope, he still knew that an abrupt emancipation would cause social chaos and he did not want to betray his own good judgment.

Eventually, Lincoln decided to issue a *partial* Emancipation Proclamation. Notice the word "partial". It came after months of strongly divided advice from his cabinet. Lincoln waited for the most strategic time to issue it and eventually, on January 1, 1853, he decided the timing was right and issued his Presidential Emancipation Proclamation. He said it was unconstitutional but necessary as a "war measure." It, he was told, would be a useful instrument to wage war. It was a craftily designed political measure. His Proclamation declared that all slaves in the South under Confederate control were free but all the slaves in States, or sections of States, that were under Union control would remain slaves. In other words, people loyal to the Union could keep their slaves. Secretary of State Seward ridiculed Lincoln's hypocrisy: "We show our sympathy with slavery by emancipating slaves where we cannot reach them (rebel territory) and holding them in bondage where we can set them free (Union territory). The *London Spectator* said: "The principle (of the Proclamation) is not that a human being cannot justly own another, but that he cannot own him unless he is loyal to the United States."

Did most of the people in the North greet the President's Emancipation Proclamation with great joy and jubilation? Mrs. Goodwin wrote: "In cities and towns all across the North, people had anxiously waited for word of Lincoln's action (regarding the Proclamation) . . . . Finally, at roughly 10 pm . . . a man raced through the crowd . . . Douglas would long remember the 'wild and grand' reaction, the shouts of 'joy and gladness,' the audible sobs and visible tears. The happy crowd celebrated with music and song." That seems to give us the impression that the Proclamation was welcomed with enthusiasm by most people all over the North. I say "baloney." Later on, Mrs. Goodwin gives us the other side; she describes some of the backlash to the Proclamation. How was it received by the majority of people and the troops? It had little impact on the South where most slaves continued working on plantations for their masters (now often only women) due to their loyalty and/or the simple fact that the plantations provided their only security, work, food, and housing. The partial Proclamation's impact on the North and the Union troops was profound in negative ways.

Another historian, Thomas J. Di Lorenzo, gives his version of the story. He gives us a broader, more revealing, and, I believe, a more accurate description: "Most Northerners in 1863 were shocked and surprised by the Emancipation because they had not been told by their government that they were fighting and dying by the tens of thousands for the well-being of black strangers in faraway states where most Northerners had never been. Hostile white immigrant mobs had assaulted blacks in Northern cities for decades." Colonel Arthur Fremantle wrote: "The people who can't pay $300 (to get out of the draft) naturally hate being forced to fight in order to liberate the very race who (sic) they are most anxious should be slaves. It is their direct interest not only that (sic) slaves should remain slaves, but that the free Northern Negroes who compete with them for labor should be sent to the South also." (Remember; it was a rich man's war and a poor man's fight. Doesn't that sound familiar?)

Desertions of Union soldiers rose rapidly after the partial Proclamation was issued. (Desertions of Confederate soldiers rose toward the end of the war when they realized that the war was lost and that to continue fighting and dying could not bring victory.) Worrying about the escalating number of men deserting from the Union army, Lincoln asked Sergeant J. L. Stradling to honestly tell him how the rank and file feels about matters. The Sergeant said: "Mr. President, I approach the Emancipation Proclamation with great reluctance, for I know how your heart was set on issuing that document. (The soldier was incorrect about Lincoln's decision being issued with his heart set on it. <u>This is an example of how early and easily the myths began.</u>) So far as I am personally concerned, I heartily approve of it. But many of my comrades have said that if they had known the war would free the niggers they would never have enlisted, so many of them deserted. Others said they would not desert, but they would not fight any more."

The Union enforced the conscription; the necessary number of troops was drafted, the war was fought and the Union won. Confederate troops went home to a broken, devastated, barren, and financially bankrupt South and the harassment of military rule. Union troops went home to a North greater in population than before the war. They came home to Andrew Carnegie, J. P. Morgan, corporations rich from war profits, and monopolies of industries and railroads, and a burgeoning under-class of under-paid, disadvantaged, and badly mistreated workers in coal mines, shoe factories, and other industries. I will give you some examples.

If differences between sections of the country could have been settled without a war, would the seceded States return to a friendlier and less coercive Union and would freedom from slavery and the integration of the races have been accomplished in a wiser and better way for the black race? Was there another and better way to settle the conflicts between the sections and emancipate the slaves? Some historians tell us how other nations did it in much the same way that Lincoln once thought was best; and I do not mean colonization. How can we know what the US would be like today if another course was followed and the war was never fought? What if States were allowed to secede? Would States eventually freely choose to be part of a Union that gave them freedom of choice? Would most, perhaps all, States want to be part of a strong, fair, prosperous, just, reasonably equitable, and free nation?

I hope my documentation provides abundant proof for my assertion that the black race is deceived if they believe that Abraham Lincoln and the common people in the North went to war to free the slaves and that the Southern troops fought to keep their slaves. Plantation slavery was destined for extinction by changing economic and social circumstances. Could two nations, the Union and the Confederate States, have existed side by side and, become two great nations; or, given time, find peaceful solutions to sectional problems that would have brought them together again; voluntarily and without force? Slavery was headed for extinction without the war.

CHAPTER SIX

THE SECOND CIVIL WAR
ALIAS
"RECONSTRUCTION"

Statewide elections in Louisiana in 1872 polarized the state, with Republican and Democratic candidates both claiming to have won the governorship. A Federal judge ruled in favor of the Republicans, and Grant ordered troops to enforce the judgment. Louisiana whites refused to accept the verdict and formed organized resistance supported by armed paramilitary units known as White Leagues. The Red River town of Colfax was the county seat of Grant Parish. Racial hostility in the parish was long standing, with Union appointed black officials in control. Union militia and militant black men guarded the courthouse to protect Union installed county officers. On Easter Sunday, 1873, the White Leagues attacked the Union troops and militant blacks with rifles and small artillery and eventually overpowered them. When the fighting ended, over a hundred blacks and two white men were dead. A federal grand jury indicted seventy-two whites and three were convicted. Later on, the Supreme Court overturned those convictions. This was one of the skirmishes and battles stemming from the Congressional Reconstruction that ushered in our second Civil War.

Of all the historians I have read, my favorite foil is the carefully politically correct Professor Anne Sarah Rubin's *A Shattered Nation: The Rise and Fall of the Confederacy*. She described reconstruction as "benign" and the Union soldiers as mostly "magnanimous" when they entered homes of the conquered South without an invitation. That is much different from the way my maternal grandmother (who was there) talked about it. Professor Rubin must know zilch about Lincoln's fight against radical Republicans and their venomous Congressional Reconstruction. Lincoln tried hard to prevent it. To me, Rubin's bias is laughable. She seems to me to be obsessively interested in the "manhood" and masculinity of Southern soldiers. It makes me wonder about her psyche.

Lincoln's true greatness was never clearer or brighter than it was when he spoke after his second election and when he spoke after Lee's surrender. He begged for kindness and understanding for all of the nation, including the South, when he said: "With malice toward none; with charity for all; with firmness in the right as God gives us to see the right, let us strive on to finish the work we are in; to bind up the nation's wounds; to care for him who shall have borne the battle, and for his widow, and his orphan—to do all which may achieve and cherish a just, and a lasting peace, among ourselves, and with all nations." He clearly wanted healing and reconciliation for his nation. I found no expression of any desire that Lincoln had to punish and humiliate the defeated section of his nation. He suffered and believed that all of the common people in the South had already suffered too much. The radicals disagreed. Lincoln said: "There were men in Congress who, if their motives were good, were nevertheless not practical, and who possessed feeling of hate and vindictiveness in which he did not sympathize and could not participate. He hoped there would be no persecution, no bloody work, after the war was over."

Historian Benjamin Thomas wrote: "It distressed the President that men of his own party sought revenge upon the South. None of the representatives of the restored state governments had been allowed to take seats in Congress. The Wade-Davis bill had been reintroduced in the last session, and though it had been decisively defeated, there was much talk of ruthless confiscation, of mass disenfranchisement of Southern citizens, of treating the Southern states as conquered provinces."

When Lee surrendered at Appomattox, General Grant displayed respect for Lee and the Confederate army. The terms of surrender were lenient and designed for reconciliation. The terms allowed Confederate officers, after relinquishing their arms and artillery "to return to their homes, not to be disturbed by the United States authority, on the condition that they never take up arms against the Union until properly exchanged." Grant believed: "It would be an unnecessary humiliation to call on them to deliver their side arms." He inserted a provision allowing officers to take their side arms, as well as their private horses and baggage." He also allowed Confederate troops, who were not officers, to keep their horses that he said they would need to rebuild and plow their farms.

The new Louisiana constitution emancipated all slaves within the State and provided "the benefit of public schools equally to black and white" and ratified the thirteenth amendment. The State voluntarily demonstrated its desire to cooperate, satisfy Union wishes and become reconciled with the Union. Lincoln wanted to allow the governments of Louisiana, Virginia, and South Carolina to convene and govern their States. The radicals in congress fiercely opposed Lincoln's action. Radical opposition became so strong that Lincoln yielded and issued an order rescinding his first decision and prohibiting the South Carolina and Louisiana governments from convening.

Historian Carl Sandburg tells us about a conversation between Lincoln and General Sherman. The Union victory was evident and Sherman asked Lincoln: "What was to be done with the rebel armies when defeated? And what should be done with the political leaders such as Jefferson Davis?" Sherman said: "All he wanted of us was to defeat the opposing armies, and to get the men composing the Confederate armies back to their homes, at work on their farms and in their shops?" He suggested that the best thing for Jeff Davis was to clear out and escape the country.

Lincoln's first speech after Lee's surrender was lengthy and he made a strong plea for peaceful reunion. He said that the reintroduction of Southern states into the Union was "the greatest question ever presented to practical statesmanship." Lincoln spoke directly about his controversy with radicals regarding Louisiana; clearly explaining his desire for reunion with seceded States without punishment.

In his speech, Lincoln said: "The amount of constituency, so to speak, on which the Louisiana government rests, would be more satisfactory to all, if it contained fifty, thirty, or even twenty thousand, instead of only about twelve thousand, as it does. It is also unsatisfactory to some that the elective franchise is not given to the colored man. I would myself prefer that it were now conferred on the very intelligent, and on those who served our cause as soldiers. Still the question is not whether the Louisiana government, as it stands, is quiet all that is desirable. The question is 'Will it be wiser to take it as it is, and help to improve it; or to reject and disperse it' Can Louisiana be (sic) brought into proper practical relation with the Union *sooner* by *sustaining*, or by *dissecting* (italics mine) her new State Government?'

"Some twelve thousand voters in the heretofore slave-state of Louisiana have sworn allegiance to the Union, assumed to be the rightful political power of the State, held elections, organized a State government, adopted a free-state constitution, giving the benefit of public schools equally to black and white, and empowering the Legislature to confer the elective franchise upon the colored man. Their Legislature has already voted to ratify the constitutional amendment recently passed by Congress, abolishing slavery throughout the nation. These twelve thousand persons are thus fully committed to the Union, and to perpetuate freedom in the state—committed to the very things, and nearly all the things the nation wants—and they ask the nations recognition, and its assistance to make good their committal. Now, if we reject, and spurn them, we do our utmost to disorganize and disperse them."

"We in effect say to the white men 'you are worthless, or worse—we will neither help you, nor be helped by you'. To the blacks we say 'This cup of liberty which these, your old masters, hold to your lips, we will dash from you, and leave you to the chances of gathering the spilled and scattered contents in some vague and undefined when, where, and how'. If this course, discouraging and paralyzing both white and black, has any tendency to bring Louisiana into proper practical relations with the Union, I have, so far, been unable to perceive it."

"If, on the contrary, we recognize, and sustain the new government of Louisiana the converse of all this is made true. We encourage the hearts, and nerve the arms of the twelve thousand to adhere to their work, and argue for it, and proselyte for it, and fight for it, and feed it, and grow it, and ripen it to a complete success. The colored man too, in seeing all united for him, is inspired with vigilance, and energy, and daring, to the same end. Grant that he desires the elective franchise; will he not attain it sooner by saving the already advanced steps toward it, than by running backward over them? Concede that the new government of Louisiana is only to what it should be as the egg is to the fowl, we shall sooner have the fowl by hatching the egg than by smashing it."

If the radical politicians listened to Lincoln, there would have been no need for the bloody fights in Colfax, New Orleans, and other places. Lincoln clearly pled for tolerance and friendly relationships but radical politicians would not heed his wisdom. Louisiana was a test case. Would the nation now turn away from force and coercion necessary to win the war and turn to friendly cooperation and persuasion? Or will radical politicians insist on a second civil war?

General Grant (while he was still a General) believed that the Lincoln view had behind it "the great majority of Northern people, and the soldiers unanimously." Sherman had the identical opinion. Noah Brooks said: "A large majority of the people (North and South) approved of Lincoln's speech. Reunion was then the foremost thought in the minds of men" Lincoln said: "None need to expect that he would take any part in hanging or killing even the worst of them . . . Enough lives have been sacrificed. We must extinguish our resentments if we expect harmony and union." The abolitionist, Horace Greely, pled for "universal amnesty and reconciliation with the gentlemen of the South."

Lincoln's assignation was the worst blow that could have been dealt to the hopes of the South. Lincoln opposed revenge minded men and when his successor, Andrew Johnson (who had called the South "odious" and had radical views when he was Vice President) took office, he tried to follow the lenient policies of Lincoln. He took the position that the act of secession was unconstitutional and the seceded States still belonged to the Union because they were never legally out of it. He tried to leave rights and responsibilities in the hands of the States. On May 29, he issued an Amnesty Proclamation that granted full amnesty and pardon for participation in the rebellion for all Confederates except members of certain specifically excluded groups, provided the person took an oath of future loyalty to the United States and promised to support emancipation. Wendell Phillips, Charles Sumner, Thaddeus Stevens, Benjamin Wade, and other radicals were furious. In his speech to the reconvened Congress, President Johnson said that the military government forced on the South would not "restore affection" but would "envenom hatred" by its divisive character. He was so right.

Common people in the North did not want a second civil war; they did not want the first one. Jean Edward Smith, author of *Grant*, admitted that: "The Northern commitment to black equality had never been deep." One Republican wrote: 'The truth is our people are tired out with this worn out cry of 'Southern outrages' . . . Hard times and heavy taxes make them wish the 'nigger, everlasting 'niggers', were in hell or Africa."

After President Hayes took office, Ari Hoogenboom said: "(President) Hayes knew that Northern opinion would not long sustain the troops in the South." *The New York Evening Post* predicted that: "Its (troop removal and strife) disappearance would give even greater satisfaction to the people of the North than to those of the South." When Hayes was elected

President, he, like Lincoln, wanted reconciliation of the sections. Some Northern Republican newspapers and radical congressmen were furious and condemned the withdrawal of troops and called Hayes a traitor. Their fear was that the South would become solidly Democratic and threaten their control of the government—which it eventually did.

Most of the common people in the North did not hate white people in the South. They were apparently influenced very little by the castigation of Southern white people by loud abolitionists and radicals. Northern laymen never called for vengeance or punishment. There are many accounts of Union and Confederate soldiers having friendly conversations and exchanging coffee and tobacco during the war when they were away from the fighting. Radical politicians insisted on and prosecuted their "Congressional Reconstruction" and the South became an occupied territory for a decade.

Radicals like Sumner and Chase believed that the vote should be immediately given to all black people and that suffrage should be mandated; that rebel leaders should be punished, and the federal government should assume control of the seceded states. They should exercise *sole* control, "treating the rebel organizations and government as absolutely null and void." This time the radicals used the guise of protecting black people and working to enforce the abolition of the slaves to justify and hide their primary goal; which was to grab and keep political control of the South.

Union troops were ordered to remain in the South to ensure the election of Republicans and the placement of black men in State and Federal offices. Congress would not seat Senators or Representatives from Confederate States while Andrew Johnson was in office. Radical Republicans had complete control of Congress. Over the strong objections of President Johnson, the radical Congress passed a Reconstruction bill that extended the lifetime and jurisdiction of the Freedmen's Bureau for an indefinite period of time and strengthened a system of quasi-military courts to enforce its decrees, and the authority to function anywhere in the country. On February 19, Johnson returned the bill with a veto. He argued that, for the benefit of blacks, the bill took land from former owners without legal process and that it authorized Congress to spend money on blacks in ways never considered proper for whites and . . . "**A system for support of indigent persons in the United States was never contemplated by the authors of the constitution—nor can any good reason be established why, as a permanent establishment, it should be**

founded for one class or color of our people more than another." Now you know when, where, how, and why the first public welfare programs began.

Johnson vetoed the first two radical acts of Congress and his first veto was sustained but his second was overridden. With many pardons and with proclamations, Johnson tried to bring the seceded States back into the Union on friendly terms. Radicals fought every conciliatory action of Johnson and insisted on a vendetta. On May 13, 1870, Congress passed three Acts of Enforcement that were eventually declared unconstitutional by the Supreme Court.

United States v. Reese was a voting rights case. The Court invalidated the operative sections of the Enforcement Act of 1870, holding that the Fifteenth Amendment did not confer the right of suffrage in state and local elections. The Constitution gave determination of rights of suffrage to the States.

In *United States v. Cruikshank*, the Supreme Court determined that the Fourteenth and Fifteenth amendments applied only to action by the States, not by individuals. "The power of Congress to legislate does not extend to the passage of laws for the suppression of ordinary citizens within the States. That duty was originally assumed by the States; and it still remains there." (This decision was later overturned making Federal Civil Right laws supreme over State laws.) In the *Cruikshank* decision, the Supreme Court tried to prevent the attempt of the Federal government to abrogate the power and authority of State and local governments. The *Nation* described the Acts like this: "They not only increase the power of the central government, but they arm it with jurisdiction over a class of cases of which it has never hitherto had, and never pretended to have any jurisdiction whatsoever." The rise of Imperialism in America had a full head of steam in the first years of "reconstruction" and the second Civil War became overt and hostile. Soon troops of the Union army, Union officials, and militant blacks met organized resistance in the South.

When General Grant became President Grant, the leopard changed its spots. In early May of his first term, President Grant ordered troops in the South to take the field, help federal officials, and maintain Republicans in Southern political offices. President Grant sent General Sheridan to Louisiana to oversee elections with orders that gave him a "military blank check." The Louisiana legislature was set to convene January 4, 1875. When the legislature convened, the Democrats controlled the House and seated five Democrats from contested districts. General Emory, under orders from General Sheridan, dispatched a detail of troops to clear the House chamber of all persons who could not produce election certificates. The five newly elected Democrats were forcibly ejected, at which point the remainder of the Democrats stalked out in protest. The Republicans then organized the House and elected a speaker. Attorney General Amos T. Ackerman said: "These combinations (of Southern resistance) amount to war, and cannot be effectively crushed on any other theory." The army acted and suspended the writ of habeas corpus.

On November 14, 1864, Lincoln wrote to General S. A. Hurlbut: "Few things, since I have been here, have impressed me more painfully than what, for four or five months past, has appeared as bitter military opposition to the New State Government of Louisiana." Friendly cooperation, persuasion, and peaceful reunion were never in the minds of radicals. The second civil war guaranteed the eruption of riots and bloody fighting. "In New Orleans troops and black militia commanded by General Longstreet fought a pitched battle with 3,500 White Leaguers intent on seizing the statehouse and overturning the government. Longstreet lost eleven killed and sixty wounded, the White League suffered 21 dead and nineteen wounded. The White League took the statehouse and installed a rival Democratic government. Republican office holders took refuge in the United States customhouse. The next day, Grant issued a presidential proclamation and sent five thousand troops and three gunboats to New Orleans.

General Sheridan wired Grant to declare the White Leaguers "banditti" and he could prosecute them as such. The press got hold of the wire. Radical Republicans were elated. The radical press said: "Crush them utterly, remorselessly." Moderate Carl Schurz called Sheridan's proposal: "So appalling that every American citizen who loves liberty stands aghast." William Cullen Bryant said Sheridan should "tear off his epaulets and break his sword and fling the fragments into the Potomac." A committee was appointed and Democrats were awarded control of the House and Republicans control of the Senate in Louisiana.

When Rutherford B. Hayes became President, he knew the vast majority of the Northern population was fed up and wanted the troops withdrawn and back home. On April 10, 1877, after a controversy in South Carolina, Hayes "withdrew troops from the statehouse, but not from the State lest he admit that they had been there without sanction of law." Radical Republicans were inflamed. The *New York Times* called the withdrawal of troops a "surrender".

Let me ask you to put yourself in the shoes of people who experienced the war and years of Reconstruction and ask yourself how you would feel.

If you were a Union soldier on duty in a Southern State, would you want to be away from home a decade after the first war or would you rather be back at home? If you were a kind hearted soldier, would you take advantage of an opportunity to mistreat or harm a Southern man, woman or child? I do not believe that you would. If you were mean, selfish, and cruel, like a minority (hopefully, a small minority) of a large number of soldiers in a similar situation always are, would you go into homes without an invitation and take whatever you wanted, and behave in ways to insult and intimidate the residents? Yes, you would. I would not accuse any Union soldier of raping women unless I had definite proof; but I do have proof.

War raises aggression and other base emotions in warriors and lowers a man's control of his emotions, especially aggressive and sexual passions. While Camp Livingston was still under construction, a row of make-shift buildings was erected along a stretch of the highway just outside the gates of the camp. They were used for bars, liquor sales, and prostitution. It always happens. When I was in Hawaii in 1944, military men formed lines waiting to enter houses of prostitution. I lined up; went into a room, and when the prostitute entered, I said: "Thanks, but no thanks, and left."

The robbery, assaults, and rapes of civilian women and children by civil war soldiers occurred in Southern States, more than the Northern but it was not because Union troops were more immoral and meaner than Confederates. The percentage of sociopaths would be about the same in both armies. There were more rapes in the South simply because Union troops were in the South much more often and longer than Confederate soldiers were in the North. I am not saying, and I do not believe, that more Union soldiers were rapist and criminals than Confederates soldiers. Union soldiers simply had more opportunities for offences against civilians than Confederate soldiers. I want to believe that the percentage of criminals was small in both armies.

Dr. Thomas P. Lowry, in his book, *The Story The Soldiers Wouldn't Tell,* researched the records of military trials. Most of the records of

Confederate trials had been burned. He researched the court-martial records of Union soldiers and said: "A survey of less than 5 percent of the Federal court-martials, preserved in the National Archives, has yielded more than thirty trials for rape." If the same proportion of rapes was in the 95 percent that was not researched then the total number of rapes in the South would be more than 2,800. Black and white women were victims and black women were raped more often than white. Abuse of black women and the destruction of plantations, that blacks depended on for food and a place to live, helps to explain the reasons why many Southern black people hated Union soldiers. When the news of these atrocities spread to the general public, they frightened black and white Southern people. Dr. Lowry documents a number of the cases. Most convicted perpetrators were hanged or killed by a firing squad, with Lincoln's approval.

If you were a widow, or orphan, of a Confederate soldier, how would you feel about Union soldiers enforcing military rule? If you were a surviving Confederate soldier and knew that you were being branded and treated like a criminal, how would you feel? If you held a public office and the military Governor removed you and replaced you with a black man, how would you feel? The normal and natural response would be resentment, fear, even hatred, and a desire to regain control of your home.

Let me give you some excerpts from the diary of a Confederate veteran that gives us a glimpse into his experiences and feelings about Reconstruction. His name was Isaac Hermann and his writing skills tell us that he was an intelligent man with some education:

> "When the commanding officers of the confederate army surrendered and stacked arms the rank and file expected that the terms promulgated and agreed upon would be carried out to the letter . . . . The following were the terms of the agreement entered into between General Grant and General Lee: The officers and men to return to their homes and remain there until exchanged and not to be disturbed by the United States authorities so long as they observe their paroles and the laws in force in their respective states.
>
> But the fellows who directed the ship of state and who were invisible on the firing line became invincible, when the South lay prostrated. The first order was from Secretary Staunton (Sic), for the arrest of our commanding officers. This order, however, was resented by General Grant as contrary to the cartel and should not be

executed. This caused a rupture between the two and the order was finally rescinded. The next step was to disperse all State authority and appoint a military Governor. General Wilson acted in that capacity in Georgia. The same year, 1865, negroes (sic) were proclaimed free and military garrisons established in every town, city, or village throughout the South. Under the supervision of those militaries the Freedmen's Bureau was established, forcing negroes (sic) to migrate from one place to another, thus breaking up the good relationships still existing between masters and servants. The bureau was seemingly gotten up for the protection of the Blacks, as if they needed any protection, they to whom we owed so much for their good behavior during the time when every available man able to bear arms was at the front, leaving their families in charge of the negroes. The gratitude of our people was, or ought to have been, sufficient guarantee in that line.

Such harmonious condition did not suit the powers that be, there was venom in their heart for revenge, and punitive measures were concocted. Never were captives bound tighter than the people of the South. The body (delegation of South Carolina Legislators) at that time was composed of coal black negroes, mullatoes, (sic) and carpet baggers. Cartossa, a mullato, was then Trreasurer of the State. A negro named Miller was General in chif (sic) of the S. C. militia of State troops . . . some say we are progressing. That is true, but in the wrong direction. Retrogressing is the proper word to apply. . . .

Is it no wonder that the men of the South became desperate and used desperate remedies to oust more desperate diseases? The carpet baggers made their exit. The negroes' (sic) mind had been prejudiced under the auspices of those vultures. They were forced into societies, one of which was the Rising Sun. God only knows what ultimate results they expected to obtain. Drums and fifes were heard in every direction at night. The woods were full of rumors that the negroes (sic) are rising . . . .

It is a half century that has elapsed since the thunder of Fort Sumter shook this hemisphere. New generations have appeared on the scene, fraternization is progressing slowly, but surely, the past is relegated gradually to the rear and the States again assert their rights, as they see it. Therefore it behooves the National administration to see to it that equal rights to all and special privileges to none, is its duty to enforce so as to maintain this nation the greatest nation on the globe.

The sections must get together and look to the wants and needs of their associates and as far as lies in their power assist in bringing relief. Thus past differences will vanish and brotherly love will again prevail and the United States of America will forever be united to stand in bold relief the model government in the world."

There is no plan that could have been more efficient than the stupid Congressional Reconstruction in alienating the black and white races in the South. They were partially successful in inciting former slaves to turn against the white race with hostile actions; but not as successful as they wanted to be.

After the Civil War, many friendships remained in the old South and some new friendships were begun, but the prevailing atmosphere of racial relationships was poisoned by the radical Congressional Reconstruction and became more difficult and embittered (just as Abraham Lincoln had predicted they would be). During the Congressional Reconstruction, the South organized resistance to Union rule, the appointment of black men to ruling offices, and the disenfranchisement of white people. In some States, the population of black people was equal to, or larger then, the population of white people and some black men became militant and belligerent and Southern people became angry and afraid. They organized to prevent anarchy; restore social order and stability, and to ensure white control. They organized the KKK to fight actual evils with evil. Nothing can justify either evil. Again, black men and women suffered more than anyone else.

After the war, the Northern common people eventually insisted that all of the Union soldiers should be returned to their homes and, in 1877; President Hayes began the final withdrawal and all Union soldiers were withdrawn. Carpetbaggers went home, and the South was left to govern itself. Many good relationships had been poisoned. The economy and infrastructure were in shambles. There was no Marshall Plan to help the South recover. Reestablishing social stability, order, and security was the first task of white government when it regained control. Most black people in the South wisely adapted to the prevailing conditions; even though the conditions were worse than before the war for many black people. Segregation was enforced in the South. Most blacks and whites spontaneously separated themselves in social situations simply because they felt more comfortable in their own social groups and neighborhoods.

Forced segregation remained much too long in the South but we still do not know if forced integration has been more harmful or helpful to both races.

Almost all black people remained in the South after they were free to go wherever they wanted to go. There was never a mass exodus of black people from the South. Some migration to the North began only when modern machinery eliminated their jobs. They were not wanted in the North and black people believed that, even though segregated, their home and livelihood was in the South. That is where most black people could still make a living and that is where they chose to stay until the plantation economy was changed and work became unavailable. It was their home.

The eighth census in 1960 showed these pre-war numbers:

Population in Louisiana was 357,629 whites; 18,647 <u>free</u> blacks: 331,726 black slaves.

Population in Mississippi was 353,901 whites: 773 free blacks; 436,631 black slaves.

Population in Alabama was 596,431 whites: 2,690 free blacks; 435,080 black slaves.

Population in Illinois was 2,701,323 whites and 7,628 free blacks.

Population in New York was 3,831,730 whites and 49,005 free blacks.

The populations in Louisiana and Alabama were almost equally half black and half white in 1960. In Mississippi it was almost half and half with 83,500 more blacks than whites. In 1970 these three States remained about half black and half white with Louisiana and Mississippi having more blacks than whites.

In 1960, New York had a .01 percent black population and Illinois had .005 percent black population—if my math is correct.

The ninth census, the census in 1970, five years after the Confederates surrendered, revealed these numbers:

The population in Louisiana was 362,000 whites and 364,210 blacks.

The population in Mississippi was 382,806 whites and 444,201 blacks.

The population in Alabama was 521,384 whites and 475,510 blacks.

The population in Connecticut was 527,549 whites and 9,668 blacks.

The population in Illinois was 2,511,096 whites and 28,762 blacks.

The population in New York was 4,330,210 whites and 52,081 blacks.

The 1970 census also said: "(Blacks) Drawn largely from the plantations, where their increase was natural, rapid, and sure, to cities and camps, where want, vice, and pestilence made short work of the multitudes hastily gathered, inadequately provided for, and left for the first time to their own control, while so much of the impulse to procreation as depended on the profits of slave breeding was withdrawn by the abolition of chattelism, it is only to be wondered at that the colored people of the South have held their own in the ten years since 1860."

What do these numbers prove? Was the treatment of the black race so horrible on the plantations that they fled from the plantations and the South as soon as they were emancipated and free to leave? They did not! They remained for many years where they had a home and employment—black people who were displaced by the Union invasion had an especially hard time if they could not return to the plantations. The employment of the former slaves disappeared when machinery was invented to pick cotton, plow the ground, and do other work that required manual labor. Only after that did a slow migration begin of black people to the North to find work.

It is simply not a fact that most slaves on plantations were treated worse than the low class of people in the North. Their living conditions were far from ideal but they had a bed to sleep on, a roof over their head, food rations, their own gardens, and fresh water. None of this made slavery right but the living quarters of most slaves were better than Lincoln's log cabin. I might add that for a few of my teen years, my home was more crowded with people than a slave's cabin. My parents had six children of their own and took in two of my mother's young nephews whose parents had been killed in a fire. Add my grandmother, and that is eleven peopl in a three bed room house with one bath. I slept just fine on an army cot.

The treatment of slaves by an owner who was a cruel person was, of course, cruel. However, it is a gross mistake to assume that most plantation masters were cruel people. Some plantation owners took pride in the work and behavior of their slaves. The word "ownership" is usually odious when it applies to humans. However, good owners knew that it was wise, and better for everyone, to keep their slaves as healthy and contented as possible. Friendly relationships between owners and slaves were common because they were in the best self interest of the owner, as well as the slave. Do we believe that George Washington and Thomas Jefferson mistreated their slaves? If the story about Sally Hemming is true and she had it to do all over again, would she still want to be Jefferson's mistress and have his children? I think she would; and her ancestors would have more reason to be thankful and proud than to be ashamed.

Before the war, Senator Jefferson Davis and Senator William Seward were close friends and Seward spent many hours at the bedside of Davis during a long illness. Seward became Secretary of the State and Davis the Confederate President. Davis made a long speech on his last day in the Senate describing how wrenching and painful it was to leave his friends in Congress. He was never described as an awful man until the war began.

Before the war, Davis owned a plantation in Mississippi that he called Brierfield because it had hundreds of briar bushes. During the first year on his plantation, his twenty one year old bride died of malaria and Jefferson barely survived it. (I am not certain because I only have pages that I copied from a book but I am almost certain that the following quotes are from an essay written by Gore Vidal. "Over the next few years, Davis turned Brierfield into a successful cotton plantation that eventually (1860) had 106 slaves . . . . He developed Brierfield with the help of his slaves with whom he had a close relationship and was a benevolent master. He and his brother, Joe, were good to their slaves, lenient in discipline and always mindful of their welfare." Davis allowed his slaves to travel alone to places like Natchez and New Orleans and trusted them to return; which they always did. He set up a courthouse for slaves where only slaves judged other slaves for rule infractions. Slaves were encouraged to read and the fastest learners were rewarded. Davis encouraged his slaves to grow food for their own table and sell surplus food at local markets.

Briergate became the first plantation to build a hospital for its slaves and hire a full time nurse. Davis paid a dentist to give his slaves and regular examinations and hired a minister to preach to the slaves and his family.

He played with the children of slaves and treated them as his own children. When a slave girl married, Davis bought her an expensive wedding dress and paid for a party to celebrate the wedding. Other plantation owners said that if you want to see the latest Paris fashions you need to look at Jefferson Davis' slave women. The black people on his plantation were slaves only in their legal status because their relationships with Davis became voluntary. Davis' benevolence was exceptional but was closer to the norm than the cruelest owners. Statistics prove that many slaves were freed by their owners before and during the civil war and gave them the option of staying or leaving. The largest number, by far, chose to stay. Some slaves were dispersed when Union troops over ran their plantation and owners fled.

I am not saying that the institution of slavery was good but I am saying that it is a myth that all slaves were mistreated by their masters.

CHAPTER SEVEN

HUMANIZING SLAVES

On November 4, 2011, my newspaper had a story about Dr. David Livingstone. Livingstone was in Zanzibar; a hot bed of slave kidnapping and a hub of slave trade. The article said: "The field diary makes clear that Livingstone—an ardent abolitionist—was horrified by the moral character of the freed slaves sent to reinforce his expedition. He describes them as 'senseless slaves with no honor'. In Livingstone's account, they emerge as rebellious and violent—at one point he confides that 'if they go anywhere I must go with them or murder is certain'."

Were all slaves brutes when they arrived in America? I don't think so. My guess is that some slaves may have been brutes but the character of most slaves, by far, were not even close to brutish. They were not civilized by Western standards when they arrived, and were not the kind of Christians that most of them soon became. We can be certain that they were not all the same. Most slaves became civilized remarkably fast and the rapid rise of the black race in just two or three generations is certainly remarkable and amazing.

I refuse to accept the common idea that the character of all plantation slaves was debased before or after they became slaves. I refuse to believe that slavery obliterated the spirit, the will, the fortitude, and the personal goodness and strength of all slaves. Overcoming severe adverse circumstances required heroic achievements, but I want to believe, and I do believe that some, hopefully most, slaves made good achievements. I do not accept the idea that all black people were incorrigible brutes before they became slaves and remained that way. They were good and bad human beings with their own culture, values, and personal qualities before and after they became slaves.

Historians usually talk about slaves as one indistinct homogenous glob of people. This is a disservice that dehumanizes and depersonalizes individual slaves. Slaves were individuals with widely varied character, talents, and skills; including coping abilities. When historians stereotype slaves and disregard them as individuals, they present a demeaning characterization of a whole class of people and fail to recognize the remarkable character and achievements of many slaves. Historians also fail to tell us the fact that many slaves made valuable contributions to our American culture. The stereotype negates character and individuality. The abolitionists debased slaves when they portrayed them as a monolithic object of shame and pity. Of course, the living conditions and treatment of many slaves were pitiful but if slaves could speak from the grave, I believe they would tell us that they would much rather have our respect than out pity. Pity belittles the pitied and does nothing to lift a person. Slaves were individual human beings and, like all the rest of us, some could see themselves as more of a success than a failure as a person.

How did plantation slaves cope? Their existential circumstances were different and some conditions were harder to cope with than others, but I believe many were able to cope much better than most people believe. What were the mental and emotional resources and coping strategy of slaves that made remarkable adjustments to their situations.

Religion was valuable to slaves. Plantation slaves learned and adopted the Christian religion on their plantations. Before they had their own churches, they learned about Christianity by attending the worship services of white churches. (I do not know if slaves working in Northern factories learned about Christianity; unless they were able to attend Christian worship services, as did plantation slaves.) Some slaves brought their native religion to the States and their religion became a mix of their native religion and Christianity. There is no doubt that religion was an important and helpful influence on slaves. Religion probably helped more than anything else, except a benevolent master.

The Wikipedia Encyclopedia says: "Enslaved Africans attended their masters' worship services, the seventeenth-century influences on Negro spiritual and work songs were traditional hymns the enslaved Africans heard in worship services . . . . At these services they would grow closer in their understanding of Christian doctrine and the role that music played in that experience." The New World encyclopedia says: "Gospel music played an anomalous role in American race relations. Black gospel was a synthesis of African-based musical idioms and traditional European Christian hymns, and came into maturity during the era of slavery." If plantation slaves and the black race obtained nothing else that was good from their years in slavery, they learned about Christianity and almost all who learned it; adopted it. Slaves had a religion that gave them comfort, solace, and hope. (I wonder if Bill Maher knew about their religion.) This is one reason why Martin Luther King, Jesse Jackson, and many other black leaders are Reverends and Christian churches played an important role in Civil Rights crusades.

Slaves had music to help them cope. Gospel music and spirituals were called "work songs" because that is what they sang while working. I hope there were no plantation owners that did not allow and encourage their slaves to learn about the Christian religion and develop their own music. Many millions of people, both black and white, are inspired by gospel music and spirituals today. There is much repetition in their songs because many could not read and the pastor sang a line and the congregation repeated the line. That kind of repetition is still predominant and modern singers of all colors now use repetition in many songs. The black race now dominates not only football and basketball; it now dominates large portions of American music and culture. The black race in America has good reasons to be proud of their heritage; including its slave ancestors.

How did the slaves cope? I believe that most slaves had a desire to cope and character.

Maurice Masterlinck said:

"It is not in her (Fate's) power to prevent the soul from transforming each single affliction into thoughts, into feelings, and into treasure she dare not profane. Be her empire ever so great over all things external, she always must halt when she finds on the threshold a silent guardian of the inner life."

Pessimists and fatalists perceive human beings as a passive sculpture carved out of stone by the external circumstances of fate. Stoic character and wisdom puts the chisel in our own hands, creating out of external reality a figure of our own choosing and the figure becomes the shape of our soul. My grandmother had to be Stoic to survive; and she did more than just survive. I want to believe most slaves had Stoic character and wisdom. Slaves were human and human beings have a power available to them that I believe is completely unique to the human species. It is the power of choice in our perceptions of external events and circumstances that enables us to turn adversity into prosperity of character. Let me explain how the Stoic philosophy works.

Epictetus was a lame slave who was treated cruelly by his master. Legend has it that Epictetus' master was twisting his leg and Epictetus told his master the he would break his leg if he kept twisting it. He kept twisting and broke Epictetus' leg. Epictetus calmly and mildly remarked: "Did I not tell you that you would break my leg?" Epictetus suffered and saw suffering all around him. He looked for a way to cope and won his freedom, educated himself, and gained the respect of his contemporaries. He was a foremost figure in erecting and spelling out a philosophy that is as valid today as it was two thousand years ago. I believe Epictetus is the best teacher and I place his authority over more prolific exponents such as the Emperor Marcus Aurelius or the wealthy courtier Seneca because he lived, defined, and recorded the philosophy.

The coping kernel of the philosophy is as profound as it is simple, and vice versa. It is not "the power of positive thinking" or "mind over matter." It is more practical and realistic. The Stoic philosophy grew out of hard times and the decaying soil of Greece and is often hi-jacked by pessimists but Epictetus will not allow pessimism. The Stoic philosophy is strong medicine prescribed for people who choose to be strong; no matter what their heritage and existential circumstances are. It puts a man's happiness and well-being in his own hands more than fate or external facts.

The most valuable wisdom of the Stoic philosophy is that it explains how we can be empowered by having choices in our perceptions of external circumstances. If we know and believe that we have choices of our perceptions, that belief can transform a person's feeling and belief from helplessness into awareness of his cerebral and emotional powers over fate and external reality; even though external facts remain the same. It is hard for many people to believe that we can make choices in our perceptions of external facts, and will accept responsibility for our choices. Many slaves never knew the philosophy by name, but became Stoics in the highest and best sense of the word. They exemplified the power of the philosophy. I am not suggesting that they knew they were embracing a certain kind of philosophy. That is not necessary for anyone who is empowered by Stoic choice and resolve.

The philosophy does not deny the existence of reality as does a Christian Scientists. If you have a toothache, Epictetus does not tell you that the tooth and the pain do not actually exist. He does not say that it's all in your mind. Epictetus tells us that both the tooth and the pain are real. He would not tell a slave that he is not a slave, or that hard work is not actually hard. He does not want us to pretend that pain and misfortune are illusions, or that a person can be completely impervious to any of it. He teaches us that our mind can mold, shape, color, judge, and qualify the external facts. The mind has choices of how externals events are perceived. Different people will make different choices and have different perceptions of the same external realities.

One man may see a woman across the room and perceives her as warm and approachable and will go over and talk to her. Another man can see the same woman in the same room at the same time and perceive her as cold and haughty and will avoid her. One person can have a fender bender accident and perceive it as a catastrophe; another person can have the same accident and perceive it as a minor problem. Different people will perceive the same baby's smile or cry differently.

Two men can have much different perceptions of their job even though they are alike in almost every way and have the same job with the same pay at the same factory. One man will perceive his work as satisfying and desirable while the other man perceives his work as an irksome and unwanted chore. One man's perception will affect him in a positive way and the other in a negative way. We can be empowered or defeated by the perception we choose of our work.

If we are in a hard situation, the philosophy does not pretend that the situation is not actually hard; it does not deny the reality of the hardness of an external fact. Our perceptions do not change the externals but we can choose and change our perceptions of them. Our choices of our perceptions do not change external reality but they can change us. Epictetus lets us know that we have options and do not have to feel and think that we are helpless. Our power lies in knowing and believing that we have choices in our perceptions, and perceptions help make us what we are.

Here is the hitch. If we acknowledge that we have choices of our perceptions then we also acknowledge that we have responsibility for our choices. Some people do not want to accept that responsibility. They had rather hide in helplessness and blame externals for their sour personality. One man says that his boss is terrible and he is impossible to work with; and quits or gets fired. Another man says that the same boss is terrible but he knows that he can work with him; and he keeps his job. Tell the first man that his main problem for being out of work is in himself and he will be angry at you for saying he has some responsibility for being out of work. One man says that his rebellious son is so bad and hard to live with that he kicks him out of the home. Another man with the same rebellious son will say he is a problem and hard to live with, but they stay together and try to work through, or grow through, the problem. Tell a man who has a dismal view of life that he is his main problem, and he may hate you; or he may believe you and someday thank you for telling him. The power of a Stoic is available only to people who will accept the responsibility of having choices.

The early Christians were persecuted and the survivors had to be Stoic to survive. The Stoic philosophy reigned in Christendom until Peter Abelard and Thomas Aquinas came along and changed the angry God demanding human sacrifice to appease his wrath into a loving God and the real Word. The Stoic philosophy did not lose its value but it gained a new and better interpretation.

Jesus told the little band that followed him to turn the other cheek. This was not to make them virtuous; it was a matter of simple wisdom and survival. The Bible says that Jesus told us to love our enemies but my love is the most precious thing that I have to give and so I do not give it indiscriminately; as though it is not very special to my wife, children and friends. Someone has to help interpret loving my enemies.

Today, an African American man will probably be offended if someone calls him an "Uncle Tom". Plantation slaves had choices in their perceptions of their master and situation and I believe the slaves who fared the best knew that their well-being depended much on their perceptions of their master and situation. Uncle Toms may have been less heroic but wiser than slaves with negative and rebellious perceptions and attitudes. This does not in any way mean that slavery was good and does not absolve responsibility from heinous masters who were cruel

How does all of this have anything to do with Abraham Lincoln and the Black race? This is how. Slaves believed in a loving God and found comfort and joy in their religion and identified with a suffering but triumphant Jesus. They found pleasure in music and I believe many, probably most, had enough strength in their character that helped them cope. I know there are external situations so bad that no one can cope with them but I want to dispel the myth that all slaves were so defeated by slavery than none could experience some success and rise above their difficult external circumstances. If given half of a chance, most human beings can find the will and a way to overcome some of life's toughest and most painful realities. One of my fondest memories of my mother is when she was singing while working hard in the kitchen during the depth of the great depression and experiencing some extremely difficult circumstances. Certainly, some slaves were also able to do it; but I do not want to gloss over their hard times

The Stoic philosophy has pretenders who wallow in their misery and pride themselves for suffering like a martyr; when their misery is often self-inflicted. I might be a martyr for Islam because the religion offers such enticing rewards in their paradise. Isn't it hard to be around self made martyrs? My wife has even accused me of acting like a martyr. Stoic pretenders become objects of sarcasm—as well they should. W. S. Gilbert (1836-1911), in his clever poem, "To the Terrestrial Globe", describes silly Stoic pretensions:

> "Roll on, thou ball, roll on;
> Through pathless realms of space
> > Roll on.

> What though I'm in a sorry case?
> What though I cannot pay my bills?
> What though I suffer toothache's ills?
> What though I swallow countless pills?
> > Roll on.

> Roll on, thou ball, roll on;
> Through seas of inky air
> > Roll on.

> It's true I've got no shirt to wear;
> It's true my butcher's bills are due;
> It's true my prospects all look blue—
> But don't let that unsettle you—
> Never you mind!
> > Roll on.

A close comparison to the Stoic philosophy is the serenity prayer of Alcoholics Anonymous. It tells us to know what external circumstance that we can and cannot change. Change bad circumstances if we can. If it is not within our power to change them, learn how to accept the fact that we cannot change them; do not frustrate ourselves and feel like a failure by trying to change something that it is impossible for us to change; learn how to accept with serenity the external circumstance that we cannot control or change.

There is no room in Stoicism for a habitual pessimist or a Jeremiah with a brooding disappointment in the human species. Of course, Jeremiah was right; his people had become idol worshippers and sex addicts; but the human species has been a spectacular success in reproduction and survival and television with HBO and going to the moon. The Stoic philosophy is not for everyone. It is strong medicine prescribed for people who choose to be strong; no matter if he is red, yellow, black or white, rich, poor, slave, or master. Our well being, happiness, and self-worth does not depend on existential circumstances. It puts a man's happiness and well-being in his own hands more than fate or external facts. A true Stoic in pain stands firm. He does not cave in and crumble when faced with adversity; he behaves with bravery, not fear; he makes himself a victor, not a victim

I do not believe that the curse placed on Adam in the Garden of Eden was that he was going to have to work for a living. Work was not the curse; his perception of work would become his curse. (Many will stoutly disagree with that.) Perhaps the curse was also that he became a human being because, sad to say, most human beings do not like work that they have to do. Isn't that true? Most people hate work they have to do when they feel forced or coerced into doing it. This is especially true if they see no good purpose in the work. How many people hate having to get out of bed and go to work? Adam saw his work as a curse; worse than that, he saw it as punishment. It was not something that he freely chose for himself and whistled while he worked. I wonder how many "honey do" days Eve put him through. Adam lost the freedom of paradise and his work became a forced and coerced curse.

I hope you can see some validity in the possibility of a slave naturally and spontaneously becoming a Stoic without knowing that it was a philosophy. The Stoic power to overcome hard external circumstance may have been impossible for some slaves, but not all. I hate historians who stereotype all slaves as hopelessly impotent and none could overcome hard external facts and conditions in the way that the slave Epictetus could, and did. We denigrate plantation slaves if we do not think of them as individual humans with varying degrees of courage, character, and abilities—just like all humans. We stereotype and demean all former slaves if we insist on making all of them impotent victims; unless we believe victimhood made them politically correct. We have many authentic historical stories of slaves that became highly valuable, creative, innovative, and successful people.

I believe that more than just a tiny minority of slaves possessed the strength of will and character to stand tall when buffeted and challenged by fate. I believe that black people have more reason to be proud of their slave ancestors than to be ashamed of them. Their contributions to America are many; and greater than just the manual labor they performed. Their songs, music, and the uniqueness in their talents and culture are an integral and important part of American culture today. There is no reason to disown any part of *Huckleberry Finn, Tom Sawyer,* folk music, spirituals, folk tales, tap dancing, or the "Blues". I say to all black people today: "Be proud of your ancestors." They were individual human beings and important Americans who made a difference in what we are today. I feel compassion for cotton picking, music making slaves but more than that, I honor, respect, and thank them. They were not unimportant, meaningless, and impotent human beings.

Poverty and wealth,
Sickness and health,
Large crowds and isolation,
Low status and high position,
A prison cell and royal throne,
A frail old body and young man's frame,
All of them are what you make of them.
It's up to you.
Success and failure,
Pain and pleasure,
Scorn and adulation,
Warm affection and cold rejection,
A home that is empty and a home that is full,
A spouse that is kind and a spouse that is cruel,

Children that succeed and children that fail,
All of them are what you make of them.
It's up to you.

Bob

Most historians never bother to mention the achievements, heroics, and the valuable contributions of slaves to America. My belief that many slaves are entitled to a high opinion comes from growing up with, being with, and working beside many black men in circumstances close to slavery. They deserved and received my respect. I admired numerous black people that I knew personally, even though I was ignorantly prejudiced against the race, as a race. I am giving overdue recognition to good individual human beings who deserve respect.

Many of my heroes are now black people. We make a mistake if we think that only white people or Asians can accomplish certain things. Different races may be especially gifted in different ways and I would love to be a rap artist adored by teenage girls and could be sixty years younger; but am grateful I could be a half-decent psychotherapist. Am I jealous of many people who did things I could not do? You bet I am. I watched a black artist playing Gershwin's music on a piano with a Philharmonic Orchestra a few nights ago and he put goose bumps up and down my spine.

CHAPTER EIGHT

MODERN SLAVERY

AND

THE WAR ON BLACKS

A recently published book, written by Star Parker, has the title *Uncle Sam's Plantation: How Big Government Enslaves America's Poor And What We Can Do About It.* I looked it up on Amazon and found that Star Parker is a black woman who has lived what she writes about. She makes the case that many poor people in America have sold their souls and independence for public welfare and entitlements. She demonstrates how many people are living in conditions that are similar to, or worse than, the living conditions of plantation slaves. One reviewer of the book said that governmental programs have caused the breakdown of the family unit and this is especially true in the black community and "according to the U.S. Department of Health and Human Services roughly 70% of black children are born out of wedlock . . . . If there is anyone who knows firsthand the degradation and moral bankruptcy that comes with perennial dependence on "Uncle Sam" it's Ms. Parker—she lived it."

Those are modern forms of bondage? The burdens of unemployment fall on the black race in highly disproportionate numbers. The high proportion (compared to white) of black men living in jails or prisons is an American travesty. A higher percentage of black men are arrested than any other race. Many black youths that drop out of school are more likely to be trapped in poverty. The number of black women who must raise children without a father and depend on government assistance becomes a trap. A mother on welfare is required to surrender much of her freedom and independence to receive subsistence from the government. Forced dependency makes pride hard to achieve. A disproportionate number of abortion clinics are in the center of poor black populations and some believe that it is nothing less than a form of the worst kind of practice of eugenics. Racial prejudice, that is unrecognized and denied, causes private business employers to favor white applicants. The number of poverty stricken single mother on welfare is a national disgrace. A new kind of slavery has replaced plantation slavery that has no end in sight. It is like the sneaky chains of government that de Tocqueville warned us about.

All of this is old stuff that everyone already knows; but there are some other facts that you may not be aware of.

Is the case overstated? Not if we examine the facts of imprisonment. From the *Drug Policy Alliance,* March, 2011, we find: "Mass arrests and incarceration of people of color—largely due to drug law violations—have hobbled families and communities by stigmatizing and removing substantial numbers of men and women. In the late 1990s, nearly one in three African-American men aged 20-29 were under criminal justice supervision, while more than two out of five had been incarcerated—substantially more than had been incarcerated a decade earlier and orders of magnitude higher than that for the general population. Today, 1 in 15 African-American and 1 in 42 Latino children have a parent in prison, compared to 1 in 111 white children. In some areas, a large majority of African-American men (55 percent in Chicago, for example) are labeled felons for life, and, as a result, may be prevented from voting and accessing public housing, student loans, and other public assistance." (Not to mention staying at home and helping the wife make a living and raise the kids.)

As of June 30, 2007, the incarceration rate of all people in State or Federal prisons or jails was 773 per 100,000 for white men and 4,618 per 100,000 for black men. Black people simply do not commit that many more crimes than white people. The best lawyers can be bought with enough money but the reason for so many blacks in prison is more sinister than not being able to afford a good lawyer. I believe that more than half of the budgets for all Federal, State and Local law enforcement should be taken from them and given to the Legal Aid Departments to defend the poor; but I will tell you of an even better solution a little later.

Whites use drugs five times more often than black people but 62.7 percent of all drug offenders admitted to state prisons were black and only 36.7 were white. Black men are imprisoned at a rate 13.4 times greater than that of white men. From 1985 to 1990 the percentage of black admissions to jails and prisons increased from 53% to 62% while the percentages of whites fell from 31% to 21% and it was caused primarily by drug arrests. It is grossly dishonest to try to explain the discrepancies by saying that black people use more drugs or commit more crimes than white people.

A recent television documentary exposed the illegal stop and search of black people in New York City; black men who are doing nothing but standing or walking on a street and are not behaving in any way that justifies stopping them. I have forgotten the numbers in the documentary but they were staggering. Men are made to empty their pockets, or police search their pockets and, if a small amount of marijuana is found on them, they are arrested. The police chalk up another arrest and the black man has a record and stigma on his name. I do remember that more than ninety percent of the stopped and searched people are Black or Hispanic. I found the documentary unbelievable. This kind of police behavior does not occur everywhere. I believe President Obama should give his Attorney General a good talking to and insist on his speaking to the New York Mayor and telling him to immediately stop this prejudicial nonsense. It is no wonder that black men have a low opinion of policemen.

What is the high and noble mission of the war on drugs? Simply put, it's: "Let's get those young black bastards; let's get them off the streets and lock them up." We do not have enough prisons to lock up all supposed offenders and have to keep building more prisons.

The drug war is used to justify hiring an army of jailers and drug enforcement officers. It is actually a governmental policy to keep black men locked up and keep more poor black and white women on welfare. President Obama, tell your Justice Department to stop harassing Black and Hispanic people. It is the most prejudiced institution in the nation and unjust black arrests will probably continue as long as we continue the war on drugs.

More than 47,000 people have been murdered since 2006 by drug cartels killing each other, policemen, and innocent citizens. We have spent more than $60,000,000,000 trying to stop drug smuggling into our nation and the war has been a miserable failure. It is a war that cannot be won but people who have the power to stop it; will insist on continuing the war and will not admit the fact that the war is lost. There are too many jobs and egos at stake in the DEA and ATF, and their constituency is too large for us to end the folly; not to mention influential pious people like Bill O'Reilly who spout false and dumb propaganda about drugs and drug use. That's right Bill, if a black man sells a nickel bag of pot he is a dangerous felon who should be locked up.

Many rational and intelligent people now recognize the folly and know there is only one way to end the insane war. It is a simple, common sense, and certain way to stop most of the killing, the expense, and the disastrous incarceration of a multitude of poor black and white people? It can be done by simply abolishing the laws that make the use and possession of drugs a crime and regulating drugs the same way that we do alcohol. The wisest action would be to decriminalize all drugs; but if that is too unacceptable to government and moralists, we could take a big, important, and beneficial step by just making cannabis legal. The myths used to justify outlawing cannabis (such as the myth that it is a gateway drug) will be exposed as the myths that they are. Holland has been able to close eight prisons because the crime rate dropped drastically after they decriminalized drugs. The eight prisons are no longer needed. Did we learn nothing from our experience with alcohol prohibition?

There are two principal reasons why the nation continues the futile drug war and will not listen to the rational, intelligent, common sense solution to a terrible problem. One reason is that powerful Washington Bureaus would lose much of their power, domain, and reason for an extravagant budget and thousands of drug warriors would lose their employment. The DEA and ATF will bring up their biggest guns to fight decriminalization. That should not be a problem because we could make available the sixty billion dollars to create different and better employment for them. Some could be employed in cultivating, transporting, selling, and regulating a new drug industry; which, by the way, would provide an enormous amount of tax income for governments. Thousand of drug warriors who produce nothing but costly prisoners could begin producing something beneficial and profitable.

Another strong resistance to legalizing drugs is the mistaken belief that, if a drug is made legal, it will cause many more people to become drug addicts. This is the most difficult myth to combat; the idea that if we don't keep drugs illegal, everyone will become an addict. A certain percentage of our population <u>will</u> always be addicts. The most fundamental reason why a person becomes an addict is individual psychopathology and, to some degree, cultural, much more than it is the availability of drugs. Most people are addicted to something; a little or a lot. The addiction can be for drugs, alcohol, food, sex, gambling, work, or numerous other things. Of course, some addictions are worse than others. Addiction to alcohol or food is much more hazardous to a person's health than addiction to cannabis. Very recent studies show that people who smoke pot once a week for seven years suffered no damage to their lungs.

It is incorrect to say that an addict can be cured unless you understand that when I use the word "cured", I mean an addict has become clean and sober and has found the help, character, and ways to remain clean and sober. I do not mean that the addictive personality has been excised. The personality and psychobiology that makes a person prone to become an addict remains. The compulsion can weaken over time, but it does not go away. How many food addicts have you seen cured? We have reduced addiction to nicotine with education that convinced smokers of the danger, but we did not try to make smoking a crime. The problem of obesity in our nation is increasing. Pot may be an increasing fad with young people today but no fad of young people ever lasts long; and it is a beneficial improvement if they use pot instead of alcohol.

What is the cure for addictions? Is it to make all drugs evil and illegal and to punish the addict? This is a tragic mistake that is promoted by many Evangelical Christians, and many other, mostly conservative, people. Force, coercion, or punishment has never cured an addict to anything. All attempts to cure addictions by prohibition, coercion and punishment have always failed. The cure must come from a decision within the addict that is his own unforced, not coerced, and voluntary decision. He can be influenced by love, friendship, acceptance and support but no other person can make the decision for him; it must be his. If you don't believe it, just ask any former addict who has overcome his or her addiction and has remained clean and sober. The decision must come from within the addict by his own free will and choice. He may need and ask for help to get straight; but help cannot be forced on a person. The Netherlands has far fewer problems with drug addiction than we have—and England had far fewer problems without, than with, prohibition? Prohibition and condemnation increases the compulsion while weakening the person with overloads of shame, guilt, and condemnation. Once again, let me say that force and coercion are not the answer. Prohibition produces more, rather than fewer, addicts.

Some day we may recognize addiction as a mental, emotional, and biological health and social problem and stop treating addicts as criminals.

Money saved by stopping the drug war could be used to offer treatment and other help to addicts who want it; but it cannot be forced on them. Tons of money and effort are now wasted on programs that legally compel addicts to enter treatment centers and programs against their will. It creates hypocrisy in the health practitioners who know that help cannot be forced on an addict but try to cure the addiction anyway. Good health workers can help addicts try to make the best life possible for themselves if they are not pretending to do more than help him cope with life when he is addicted.

Many religions strongly resist the decriminalization of drugs. I can already hear the loud indignation of the "conservative Christian establishment" and self righteous people, like those who railroaded the nation into alcohol prohibition. We will always have self-appointed guardians of our morals who will insist that the only answer to the drug problem is more and stricter condemnation, laws, policemen, and punishment of drug users. It is not enough for religions to make certain personal behavior a sin that can be punished in hell; they foolishly want to use legal force to prevent those behaviors. Believe it or not, my home town still prohibits the sale of alcoholic beverages but they drinks alcohol as much as anyone.

Why did our nation begin making cannabis illegal? We can blame Mexicans. Mexicans used cannabis for centuries without problems; and then they introduced cannabis into the USA. They had smoked pot for years in the same way that natives in almost every country have inhaled, drank, or chewed some kind of leaf or herb or potion to give them elated feelings, alter their consciousness, or relieve pain. Numerous religions want a monopoly on making people feel good and experience emotional and psychic highs. When Mexicans brought pot into the USA, Puritans saw how good it made people feel and they were horrified. If anything other than religion can make someone feel that good it has to be sinful.

Christians were probably the first to condemn the use of natural substances for pleasure and elevated consciousness and pain relief; with the possible exception of wine. The early Christian Church believed that only religion could morally provide emotional exaltation and consciousness altering experiences. They promoted miraculous healings, trances, speaking in tongues, and visions with religion but made the use of psychoactive leaves, herbs, potions, and drugs immoral; the work of the Devil.

The use of natural substances to alter emotions and consciousness is as ancient and universal as humans. Bill Maher will like this; the Christian religion was the first to lead the crusade to make cannabis illegal and sinful. This condemnation of a person using natural substances to experience pleasure and relieve pain is a factual attack on personal freedoms waged by many Evangelical Christians and pious moralists. Many people now suffer needlessly from depression because they are afraid of, and think there is something intrinsically wrong with, antidepressant medications prescribed by physicians; medications that have saved millions from mania, excruciating pain and depression, and prevented an unknown number of tragic suicides.

This may seem like a digression but I want to underline the fact that the drug war has unfairly and unevenly injured young black men more than any other race and I am making a plea to stop the war on blacks. Young black men are stigmatized and harmed for life when they are arrested for anything.

Bill Cosby has, and probably still is, working hard to persuade young black men to get married and stay married, and help women raise their kids. That is hard for a black man to do when he has a policeman on his tail with visions of another arrest and another black man behind bars. This is one illustration of how our first Civil War did not end all bondage of black people and how our second Civil War has given us a government that increases their bondage.

Why not stop the stupid war on young black men, now? Forgive the repetition because my feelings are strong about this. Our nation can almost immediately save billions of dollars, stop the murder of thousands of people by drug cartels, and reduce our jail and prison costs and populations by one simple act.

More than seventy percent of our expenditures for police work are used to try to control personal behaviors of people. Governments have the delusion that they can make people good by laws and force. Laws and force can prevent some bad behaviors but they cannot make anyone good. Like foolish parents, our Government believes it could and should be making personal decisions for people. Now, how many personal decisions will your eighteen year old son or daughter let you make for them?

That is another reason why we don't immediately halt the insane war on drugs. Our government is neurotic. The Nanny State is pathologically obsessed with controlling and micromanaging our personal lives with the crazy notion that they are supposed to protect people from themselves. I know that freedom is a bad word when it means freedom to harm another person; or freedom for an oligarchy to exploit vulnerable people. Freedom is bad when it is freedom from responsibility to work hard and do the right thing. Perhaps our government allows too much of the wrong kind of freedoms and too little of the right kind. Perhaps the people in our nation have become too feeble, selfish, and irresponsible to handle freedom. If that is the case, we may need a strong Dictator to whip us into shape, enforce demanding requirements on all citizens, and put some backbone back into our nation. President Obama said that we have become too soft. Is he right?

Slums can be almost as bad as prison—and prisons are worse than plantations. Most policemen want to be a good friend to black people but how can they be a friend when they have to work in the system we now have? Wouldn't it help young black and white men if many drug enforcement officers became employed as personal tutors, role models, trainers, and big brothers of young people now destined to misuse and peddle drugs? I hope policemen understand how normal it is for many black men to stigmatize them as their enemy.

Is this enough to prove the point of black and poor white bondage without having to document the number of black and poor white fatherless families trapped in poverty and unemployment and the ungodly number of children being born out of wedlock?

The North never had legal black slavery but there were many black and white slaves in the North in the 1800s and 1900s. The working and living conditions of most plantation slaves were not as harsh and dangerous as they were for coal miners in the North. In *America, 1900*, Judy Crichton, describes the working conditions in Pennsylvania coal mines: "On average, the men were getting only $250 a year (with no benefits and worked ten to twelve hours a day and six days a week) . . . . There was no American industry in which workers were subjected to more outright cheating." They worked in coal dust and "rotten gas" where they were constantly exposed to cave-ins and explosions.

Crichton has a picture of boys at work in her disclosure of the back breaking labors of mine workers. She said boys were: "Working in the breaker where coal was shattered and sorted, the 'breaker boys' worked ten-to-twelve-hour days, removing rock and slate from an endless stream of coal. Many of the boys were under the legal age of twelve; some were as young as eight or nine. Most were foreign born. Forbidden to use gloves, which would impair their sense of touch, the boys' fingers cracked and bled until the skin hardened. Many youngsters took to chewing tobacco in hopes of preventing coal dust from going down their lungs." The boys were paid one to two dollars a week.

Coal barons had a callous disregard and no concern about wages too low for adequate food. Wives and children had to eat less so the father could have enough food to keep working. The coal miners received no benefits. Their pay was too meager to provide the minimum amount of food required to maintain good health. The widows and orphans of miners killed in a cave-in or explosion received miserable compensation. Plantation owners were directly responsible for providing food, a bed, shelter, and clothing and, as you shall see, many were provided medical and dental care. Slaves who became too old to work could remain on most plantations.

In 1897, a contingent of coal miners attempted to march to Lattimore to collectively ask for better treatment and pay. Sheriff's deputies met them at the edge of the village and dispersed them by gunfire; killing nineteen men and wounding thirty-two. Three years later the coal miners had the UMW and Mitchell. They struck with organized larger numbers. The infamous Robber Barron, J. P. Morgan, who owned the banks, that owned the railroads that owned the mines, was indifferent and intransigent. The strike lasted from September 17 to October 5. The *New York Times* turned against the miners and printed rumors and lies about the strikers and a riot erupted against the miners. Eventually the coal barons, pressured by President McKinley, agreed to a ten percent raise and the miners went back to work. The best thing that happened was the formation of the union.

Shoemakers in New York, Chinese railroad workers, and practically all of the underclass workers received the same kind of pay and harsh treatment received by coal miners. Amid new wealth and splendor in the North, squalor and poverty were increasing. Writing a little more than a decade after the war, Walt Whitman wrote a scathing condemnation of economic and cultural trends in the nation. He wrote: "If the United States, like the countries of the Old World, are also to grow vast crops of poor, desperate, dissatisfied, nomadic, miserably-waged population, such as we see looming upon us of late years . . . then our republican experiment, not withstanding all of its surface-successes, is at heart an unhealthy failure." This was the United States in the aftermath of the civil war.

In 1900, Sociologist Robert Hunter did extensive research on poverty in America. Crichton tells us that Hunter, "found that millions of workers were paid so little they were unable to eat enough to maintain a state of physical efficiency . . . . in a country in which wealth is seen as a sign of God's approval, over ten million people in America were 'underfed, under clothed, and poorly housed' and he suspected those figures fell far from the truth." (Ten million unemployed in 1900 would be a much larger percentage of the population than the current 9.1 %.) Only Northern wealthy and upper class people were benefiting from the war. The aftermath of the civil war was bad for common people all over the nation.

If we compare the treatment of plantation slaves to the treatment of coal miners, we are compelled to reconsider the stereotypical vilification of plantation owners as the most and worst offenders of their workers in the nation. Plantation slavery was bad. Slavery in any form is bad. The second civil war sowed seeds of the bitterest weeds. The aftermath of the war ushered in the worst era in the history of the nation for industrial and financial monopolies, greed, graft, corruption, and working conditions for black and white people in the North and South. General Grant was a great General and a pathetic President. The war preserved the Union but revealed the greedy character of many Northern industrialists, financiers, politicians, businessmen, and much of the upper class. Andrew Carnegie was an exception. He said that he would give away all of his immense wealth before he died; and he did. J. P. Morgan was an opposite example. His treatment of the underclass was cruel, inhumane, and the rule rather than the exception.

Slavery in the North was not a legal status, but people in the North were trapped in unimaginable bad circumstances just like many people today all over the world. If we broaden our definition and understanding of slavery, we will find it today in New York and Chicago as well as Atlanta and Dallas. Our first civil war did very little to eliminate bondage, servitude, and slavery except in the legal status of the black race in America.

CHAPTER NINE

BLACK FREEDOM

Constitutional Amendments Thirteen, Fourteen, and Fifteen were passed and ratified emancipating all slaves in America. Hallelujah! The black race in America is now just as free and empowered as much as the white race. We now have no discrimination or racism in our nation of liberty, equality, and justice for all. Segregation and separation of the races are now completely relegated to the past. Doesn't almost everyone wish that was actually true?

Since the American Civil War, all racial injustice and animosity have been wiped out. There is no longer a trace of prejudice, racism, or discrimination in the mind, heart, or behavior of any American. Bondage and slavery are as extinct as the dinosaurs. No human is now used as chattel. Segregation is illegal and the black race is wholeheartedly and completely integrated into our American society. All black people are now embraced by all other races as neighbors and equal partners in business, industry, and commerce. The black race rejoices in their possession of full, fair, and equitable portions of the nation's wealth. They enjoy fair and equal opportunities in every type of employment, social organization, and education (football and basketball doesn't count). We are all embraced in brotherly friendship in one nation, undivided, with liberty and equal justice for all.

Are we really? Tell that to the highly disproportionate number of black men enjoying the pleasures of their delightful vacations in their luxurious suites in our luxurious jails and prisons. Tell that to the prisoners' wives who are struggling to raise children without a husband.

Do many people actually believe all of the baloney because they wear blinders to reality and believe what they want to believe? Factually; it is a lot of hogwash? Good people wish it was true. Bad people use racism, injustice, inequality, and poverty for selfish and political purposes. Who can say, with a straight face, that our nation is a paragon of justice and fairness? Our nation excels other countries in many ways but the poor, powerless, and disadvantaged are an ugly blight.

Martin Luther King stood on the steps of our Capitol and shouted to the cheering multitude before him: "Free at last; free at last; Thank God Almighty we are free at last." What's that? Free at last? Do you mean the black race has not been free ever since the Emancipation Amendments to our Constitution? Their legal status is free. You were surely talking about different kinds of freedom, but you were wrong Rev. King if you meant that the black race is now fully and truly free. I wish you were right, but you were wrong. Full and true freedom must encompass much more than legal status. You deserve high praise for freeing the black race from legally enforced segregation. That was a great step upward and forward, but then you made a mistake.

True and full freedom is not a mere legality? Reverend King experienced black mistreatment and disadvantages that continued after the Emancipation Amendments. He experienced discrimination. He saw a jail from the inside. He led the crusade that abolished Jim Crow laws of forced segregation. This was a huge accomplishment that increased important freedoms for black people. However, he made a huge mistake by resorting to force to try to make races integrate; the force of law.

Rev. King was probably the most authentic, powerful, and wisest spokesman for the black race that has ever lived but, like all humans, he made mistakes. The tactic he, and other black leaders, employed to lift the black race had a fundamental flaw. He betrayed the power that made him a great successful leader; the power of words, persuasion, knowledge, and appealing to the best in men. He exchanged the olive branch for a sword. Remember Peter? Did you forget that force is the opposite of freedom; and its enemy? Black leaders promoted laws to force races to integrate, whether or not they wanted to. They rightly perceived force as bad when it was used to enforce segregation. They wrongly perceived force as good when it was used to enforce integration.

King helped to abolish a bad use of force but aided and abetted a new bad use of force. Any use of force robs people of freedoms unless it abolishes laws that restrict freedoms; such as Jim Crow laws. Laws that enforce both segregation and integration deprive people of a fundamental Constitutional right; the freedom to associate, or not associate with people. Like Lincoln, he chose force to achieve the outcome he wanted in

American society and tore another piece away from our dwindling liberty and freedoms. Has forced integration lifted the black race and made our nation stronger and better?

Perhaps King's personal history made it impossible for him to believe that white people could be persuaded to do the right things. I hope that he was wrong. When we abolished forced segregation it was supposed to give all people the freedom of choice; except incarcerated people who misused their freedom. The South violated freedom when it prohibited children from having school choice or sitting in certain places on a bus. The Governor of Alabama was wrong and the Feds were right when they defended the freedom of choice. The Feds were wrong when they tried to force black and white students to be bused to and attend specific schools. We learned from that mistake and all students in the South and North now have freedom of choice. Any forced integration takes away choice and freedom.

Will a large majority of our people do the right thing only when they are forced to do it? My opinion of people is higher than that. Libertarians trust people to do the right thing and will not use force to save people from the consequences of their own behavior when it is bad. They may be too optimistic about some things but they value liberty and freedom. Authoritarians show little trust in people and resort to force quickly and often. This was a basic difference between Hamilton and Jefferson. At one point, Hamilton wanted to limit the vote to the upper class; the well educated and most intelligent citizens. He did not believe the lower class was qualified to vote. If I wanted to use the space I could quote his words to prove what I said. Different forms of government reflect fundamental beliefs in the trustworthiness of their citizens. God, I hope Christ was right.

Force is, of course sometimes necessary. It is naïve to believe that bad people will be good to us if we are just good to them. (This is an area where I believe Libertarians are naïve regarding foreign policy. It is like believing that Islam terrorists will stop hating us if we love them and are good to them. This is akin to denying the reality of evil in the world. We should try to be good to everyone who will let us be good to them but our leaders make a grave mistake if they dismiss our essential need for a strong military force in the present world circumstances.) We must have laws, policemen, and the military to protect us because some people are actually bad, cruel and malevolent and will harm unprotected people. That is the most fundamental constitutional responsibility of Government. We will always need policemen because there will always be goons, ruffians, nitwits, and sociopaths.

Everyone will agree that force can never make a bad person or a bad relationship good. Force can never <u>make</u> a bad relationship between two races good. We can never know what our country would be like today if Lincoln would have allowed States to secede. Would the South have done the right and best things about secession and slavery if they were given enough time; and learned from experience and persuasion to return to the Union and give slaves their legal freedom in a gradual, wise, and helpful way? Is there any reason why the South would not want to be in a friendly and fair Union that listened to and addressed their grievances and gave them the freedom of choice? Wise masters, like Jefferson Davis, had better workers when they were essentially voluntary workers who freely returned to his plantation. I refuse to believe that the black and white races in America must always be intransigent about race relationships and friendly relationships are impossible.

Black leaders may have held back the black race by trying to force integration. A forced relationship is, by definition, a bad relationship. King's dream was that one day no person would be judged by the color of his skin. If his dream becomes a reality, a person's color will not be a detriment or an advantage. Civil right leaders ignore that dream if they employ law to give a person advantages by the color of his or her skin. If King meant what he said, color is *not* supposed to be a consideration in people's decisions in a free and tolerant society. King would endorse the abolishment of any law prohibiting the admission of black people to schools, colleges, and universities; and I would too. Would King have approved of color being the reason for special consideration or legally required racial quotas. Neither King nor I want the color of a person's skin to hinder him. Do people want preferences because of their color?"

In our real world, color, unfortunately gives the white color advantages with some private employers. Many times a white person will be hired by a private employer instead of a black person for no reason other than color. That is bad. It has been proven; and it's wrong. Should government correct that wrong by giving preference to black people for government jobs? Wouldn't this be trying to correct one wrong with another wrong? It will naturally cause resentment in the white person with better qualifications who does not get the job. Wouldn't this also be discrimination by color? These are thorny questions.

If I was convinced that the rise in Federal control and authority was helping black people without harming the nation and all race relationships, I would be in favor of it. However, we know that laws with good intentions can have bad consequences; and it is especially true when laws subtract freedoms. It is hard to weigh the value of everyone's freedom against benefits for individuals or, even, a class of people? Preferences are supposed to help people who had suffered from long term disadvantages of being black, and they have helped numerous black young people get into college and obtain employment, and that is good. But we are still haunted by school drop outs, fatherless children, and unemployment. I am afraid that current laws are hurting, more than helping, most black people.

I called one of my nieces who taught advanced math in high school in Louisiana from the early days of integration until she retired. She told me that students have settled in and become more accustomed to and comfortable with interracial relationships and that is good. However, she also said that one high school is entirely black and it is the school that has the best facilities; and always the best football team. The other high schools have student populations that are about twenty five percent black. The races are still largely separated, but now it is by choice.

When my daughter went to high school she had the choice of going to Watson or Palmer. Palmer had a much larger percentage of black students than Watson. My daughter chose Palmer. She had a special friendship with a black basketball player who visited her in our home and she helped him with his homework. They remained friends and corresponded after my daughter went to college; however, most of her friends were white and she married a white man. My youngest granddaughter is now in the ninth grade in a Boulder, Colorado, school. In a class of more than two hundred student there are only two black students. One grade school in Colorado Springs, Colorado, has a student body that is predominantly black. Much segregation is due to locations of home but students, like most of us, usually preferred being in groups of their own race. It is a natural tendency that is demonstrated every Sunday morning in churches.

I heard Jesse Jackson on his television show complain that segregation is increasing. He doubts that it is voluntary and he is probably partly right. Economic circumstance and subsidized rent is probably one of the reasons.

He also discussed with other black leaders on his program about school drop-outs and fatherless children. They know that dysfunctional families are a primary reason why children fail in school. They talked about the value of tutors, big brothers, and role models for children and how they can help. I wish the nation would recognize the futility of the war on drugs and pay drug warriors to become tutors, coaches, big brothers, and organizers of work projects and training for poor black and white children and young people.

The voluntary segregation of groups demonstrates a normal social reality. Different cultures, more than different skin colors, are the primary reason why social groups separate themselves. The Cajuns in Louisiana were trying to organize a society to help preserve their Cajun culture when I lived in Lafayette. I hope everyone is proud of their culture and their color but our differences present another question.

Must diversity hurt unity and vice versa? A free nation will respect (which is more than tolerate) different races, cultures, and ethnic groups; it does not shun, condemn, or persecute. At the same time, strong nations need a strong core culture and language, unless it is an Empire ruled by a Caesar. We could become a nation too divided if the resistance of different cultures and languages to identify with one core culture becomes too strong. A small peaceful population, like the Quakers, could remain a separate culture and still identify with essentials of our core culture. Some cultures are now dividing the nation. Today, this is a special problem when Muslim groups are antagonistic toward our core culture.

Some people now believe that it is politically incorrect to speak of a core culture. We are faced with the dilemma of respecting diversity while protecting and fostering a strong core culture that unites us as one nation. This requires a willingness of races and cultures to accept, and be loyal to, the acknowledged core culture while retaining their unique identity. This is much more difficult now that we are much more diverse than two centuries ago. Can our nation resolve the dilemma? We know about serious conflicts and wars between ethnic groups that resort to genocide in some African countries.

How can we achieve identity and loyalty to our core culture while respecting diversity? This can occur naturally. When different colors and cultures live, work, and associate with each other often and long enough in friendly settings; prejudice and mistrust can naturally disappear. We have seen how racial prejudice has dramatically decreased among men and women in military service; and it happens in some schools. Churches and leaders of all races could foment good racial and ethnic relationships if they planned and organized social gathering where people could share music, entertainment, games and conversation in enjoyable settings and get to know each other as individuals and as we really are as persons. Churches could lead the way in planned and voluntary integration of worship services. That could make it hard for Reverend Wright to preach but I do not believe that most black pastors are like Rev. Wright.

Our educational system will hamper black freedom as long as it fails black students. Our schools are still designed primarily to prepare students for college and that is a mistake. The schools are not designed to meet the educational and training needs of students who will not go to college and a disproportionate percentage of those students are black. The entire system, not the classroom teachers, is the problem. Meaningful change is impossible until the bad system is scrapped and principals and teacher can innovate and design systems that give the most appropriate kind of education and/or training to the students they teach or train. They know their students and their potentials. They can prepare children and young people for what they want to do in life. Many black students desperately need drastic changes in the system. Teachers, I hope, are beginning to get the kind of tools and programs they need to prepare children and young people for vocations that do not require a high school diploma. Money is not the problem. (Reading and writing will always be essential skills and that should be within the reach of every normal student.)

Our educational institution is hog-tied by the Federal bureaucracy and the bureaucracy is blind or in an intentional denial of its failure. A number of manufacturing and construction companies are, at this time, unable to find the skilled workers they need. Schools can lift their students' self-esteem and teach them to think for themselves but that will not get them a job.

I hate laws that force children to attend school. They injure motivation and incentives for school attendance and learning. Children know when school attendance is compulsory; something that, like it or not, they have to do. Schools and parents have the responsibility for their children to attend school and learn and the government makes everything harder when it intrudes. Wise parents know how to motivate their children. They know children are born with an innate curiosity and desire to learn. Wise parents know how to nurture this instinct, provide interesting opportunities and challenges, and show, by example, their own interest in learning. They also know that it is best to let the child's grades be his or her grades and not the parents' and they know when it is best for them to get out of the way. Unmotivated children cannot be forced to learn; or even attend school. Forced school attendance creates a compulsive atmosphere that hinders learning but our government will not trust schools and parents and leave them alone to do their work without dumb paper work, rules, and regulations.

A law that makes school attendance and grades a matter of law enforcement is obviously ridiculous. Most children are not stupid; they can sense and understand coercion. Our schools reflect our legalistic and compulsive nation. Thank God, most schools have teachers that are good enough to motivate and teach nearly all children who have not been too badly turned off to school. Statistics tells us that our system is not working for too many black students and all of the money in the world will not help unless the system changes. My heart goes out to teachers who must work in the present system. Hopefully, some day the Federal bureaucracy will release its stranglehold on State and local school districts. A little tinkering here and there will never meet the needs of the neediest students. The Teachers' Union will also need to give up its stifling control. I believe teachers and educators will surprise us with their achievements; if given the chance.

Our "hallowed" high-priced elite universities are now little kingdoms with Princes and Princesses safely ensconced in their privileged positions. Some, who spend little time actually teaching, command high salaries and good benefits. The forty or fifty thousand dollars tuition fees are necessary only because universities insist on lavish facilities, a Country Club atmosphere, unnecessary administrators, and atmospheric packages of salaries and benefits. Most professors in our elite universities are staunch liberals in their ideas, philosophy, teaching, and politics? These schools are the prime breeders of political correctness. How did this happen? One big reason can be traced back to the 60s and 70s when radical liberal feminists made politically correct control of prestigious universities one of their highest and most important goals. They accomplished that goal with amazing success.

Political correctness and Civil Rights laws make ordinary white people as skittish as the little skinny man who married three large angry abusive women and was put in jail for bigamy. When his term was up, he begged his jailers to keep him in jail because he did not think that it was safe for him to go back out; he was afraid he may do or say the wrong thing and get another black eye. The black race cannot be blamed for the stifling atmosphere of political correctness in the nation; elite white people can take all of the credit and blame for that. Southern states suffer less from political correctness than other sections of the country and the atmosphere of black and white relationships suffers from less racial hypersensitivity and tension.

Racial relationships are better in the South because of numbers, necessity, and commonsense self interests by both races. Nearly equal black and white populations in some States presented challenges after the first civil war that never confronted the North; until black populations filled some sections of large cities. For twelve years, the formerly seceded States lived with Union troops enforcing reconstruction and the consequences were bad for black freedom. Southern black and white people fought side by side against militant blacks and Union troops after the first war. White people organized to fight organized attempts to control seats of government. The methods used by both sides were mean and ugly. The South will always wear an ugly stain from the lynching of black people and other methods used to intimidate and dominate the black race. However, they had valid reason for being afraid in 1865 of what black people may do. The number of black people that robbed, joined Union troops in armed fights, and killed white people during, and after the war was small, but it was enough to give Southern men and women realistic fears of black people. Forced segregation to insure their safety and maintain law and white control became an unfortunate necessity in the minds of white people.

Cases of atrocities against civilians are cited in Bell Irvin Wiley's *Confederate Women*. We need to remember that war brings out the best and the worst in men. Please note that I do not paint renegade Union soldiers as blacker than Confederate. Both Confederate and Union renegades pillaged, stole, and abused Southern women. I cite examples of violence only to show why white people had valid reasons for their fears of violence. The abusers were a minority and usually not under anyone's control.

On August 22, 1831, Nat Turner and seven other slaves broke into his master's home and killed all five members of the family. They went on a killing spree and other slaves joined them, killing any white person they found. By the time it was over, they killed sixty white people.

Betsy Witherspoon, the widowed cousin of Mary Chestnut, was killed by her house servants. On September 21, 1861, Mrs. Chestnut said: Hitherto I have never thought of being afraid of Negroes. I had never injured any of them; why should they want to hurt me? . . . Somehow today I feel that the ground is cut away from under my feet."

Captain Charles Wills of an Illinois regiment wrote in December, 1862: Rebels though they are, 'tis shocking and enough to make one's blood boil to see the manner in which some of our folks have treated them. Trunks have been knocked to pieces with muskets when the women stood by, offering the keys . . . all manners of deviltry imaginable perpetrated."

On December 20, 1863, a Georgia woman wrote: "Our prospects seem rather gloomy at present. I do not fear subjugation . . . but I fear the Negro."

In February, 1865, a South Carolina woman wrote: "What I most fear is not the Yankees but the Negroes . . . What will become of us? . . . Disorder has already started."

The South was fighting back to prevent riots and restore the only kind of social order that was viable. However, the violence against blacks became excessive, often unnecessary, and continued for too long. But unjust treatment of black people in the South now occurs much less than it does in large cities and other sections of the nation. Freedom from prejudice and racism and a total integration and assimilation is still far from a reality and may never become a reality in the North or the South, but the South has now improved racial relationships better than any other section of the nation. Their proximity in equal numbers made it necessary and wise to learn how to live and work together without serious racial conflict. It has been in the best interests of both races.

When I was young, Lee Street in Alexandria, a city across Red River from Pineville, was several city blocks long and was the largest black business center in the city. On Saturday nights, black people congregated on Lee Street to party, or just hang out. Some nights, some individual black men drank too much and engaged in fist fights. There was never a gang fight that I knew about. I never heard of a black gang. White teen-agers sometimes had gangs and fights between whites.

One black riot erupted on Lee Street in (I believe) the year 1943. The riot was between a company of black soldiers at Camp Livingston and local black civilians. It followed a fight between two individuals. After the individual fight was over, the soldier returned to Camp Livingston and brought a large group of black soldiers back to Lee Street and the bloody riot began. The fight was between Northern black soldiers and local civilian black men. Southern black men did not like the black soldiers. In my lifetime, I never heard of a fight between individual black and white men. I was prejudiced but all of my individual relationships with black people were always, and without exception, genuinely friendly and warm. Those relationships were heartfelt and have never ended. I wish it would have eliminated my prejudice against the race.

Today, deep bonds of affection and loyalty between black and white individuals are found in the South that no one but a Southerner can understand and appreciate. My role models in the 1930s were Cliff, Rock, and Earl; men that I worked beside in construction labor. I admired their strength and bulging muscles and I loved the way that they laughed and made fun of me when I was trying to keep up with them on the rock pile, or pushing a wheel barrow to load a cement hopper, or climbing a ladder with a roll of roofing felt on our shoulders. Cliff gave me my first nick name when I was a child. When I returned home to visit my oldest sister, my hug with the black woman who worked beside my sister in her home for half a century was as warm and genuine as was my hug with my sister. I know she genuinely loved my sister and my sister loved her. It is too easy for people to judge Southerners when they have not walked in their shoes. I had real good black friends in Louisiana; something that I have never had in Colorado or anywhere else.

Things are still far from being as fair, equal, and just as they ought to be for the black race anywhere in the nation, but the South is trying as hard as anyone to make things better. Chris and Bill, your contempt for the South is ignorant.

CHAPTER TEN

WORK VERSUS POVERTY

Everyone knows that our nation is in a bad place today and the black man bears the worst of it. Unemployment and hard times have reached a point that could be dangerous. As I write, there are public demonstrations for change spreading over the country. We know the Roman Empire's decline began with extravagant Hedonism, plebian restiveness, tyranny and extreme poverty. Our conditions are not as bad as Rome's nadir; but there are similarities. Rome tried to pacify their underclass with circuses, free bread, gladiator killings, and feeding Christians to Lions. We provide free bread, cage fighting, erotic entertainment, rappers that applaud rape and murder, and protestors that curse policemen. Rome did not fix its fundamental problems. We argue about fundamental problems and fix nothing. President Obama said we are soft. If he is right, I believe the best medicine is freedom, opportunity, and sweat on the brows of people working hard. People unemployed and idle too long become allergic to work. One of our Presidents (I can't remember which one) said, during a national malaise, "we need a nice little war." The little war we now have is not very nice. Our most urgent needs are freedom and opportunity for people to do what they once did and what they could do again.

There is an inherent danger in the poor relying on the Government for bread; it can create a class of permanent dependents and weaken our whole society. We would be cruel if we ignored the needs of the poor or falsely blame them for their circumstances. Everyone needs work for the money but they also need work to be self-reliant and independent and get out of the ditch and raise national character and morale. We see our idle population becoming angry.

Unemployment was never a problem on ante bellum plantations until machinery took away the slave's work. Some living conditions were wretched but all slaves had work and many slaves used private work to increase their income and live better than many poor white people. Some achieved a remarkable degree of self-reliance and ingenuity. Unemployment was never a problem for black men in the South until after the war.

I am old enough to remember the great depression and I saw how poverty shattered hope and crushed men and women. My family lived close to a railroad and I saw damaged men, that we called hobos, come to our door and ask for food; and my mother <u>always</u> gave them something to eat. Sometimes desperate men left home because there was no work or money and if he left home there would be one less mouth to feed when food was scarce. I was a child; but I do remember.

Some fine qualities of people also emerged and shone during the great depression. Most people, who had something to share, shared voluntarily and helped each other as much as they could. My mother gave food to black men as readily she did to white men and a black couple lived in our little barn for a while. I have never seen sharing since the depression that can match it. My parents had to struggle to provide bare essentials for our big family but were more fortunate than many because we had a cow and garden; but it was still hard to raise money to pay the rent. The depression did not divide the nation like unemployment is today. Almost everyone was in the same boat and it brought people closer together.

The current street demonstrators know nothing about hunger and depression. No one has to be hungry in our nation today. Many are protesting because they do not have as much as someone else. How little and petty can our nation become? How spoiled are our children? The pain of unemployment is real today but no one has to be afraid that his child will have no food tomorrow. However, the street demonstrators are telling us something we need to hear. The country is in trouble. That's true. But they do not have the solution.

Many people believe we must have nothing less than drastic changes in our laws and government but the question is this; does our nation have the will and courage to make drastic changes? Some people are talking about an actual revolution. That kind of change will require very strong and uncommon leaders and strong people to follow hard requirements to fix the problems. The whole damned world is in trouble; suffering the consequences of leaders asking too little from the people and the people asking too much for too little productive work; or for no work at all. Where is Elisha when we need him?

I hope street protests do not become serious riots such as those now occurring in Europe, the East, and other places in the world. The economy is not as bad as it was in the great depression. Food stamps and other programs should make possible a healthy meal on the table every day, if parents use available assistance wisely and are resourceful. If a child goes hungry it is due only to an irresponsible parent. However, this assistance does not relieve the mental and emotional pain of people desperately wanting work and unable to find it.

I have no sympathy for anyone who does not want or is not willing to work. I have no respect for social programs that provide an income for people who could; but do not want to work and help themselves. I do believe that most people want to work but our social programs are not working, and, too often, have consequences that are more harmful than helpful to individuals, families, and the nation. Some foster idleness more than they help provide and enable people to work. How can we know if a social program has more bad consequences, and do we have leaders willing to get rid of bad program? We are now witnessing the disastrous consequences of ill-advised social programs of governments all over the world that were designed to make life and work too easy. They adversely affect the character of people as well as their economy; and many agree that the USA is headed in that direction.

When Moses led the Children of Israel out of captivity in Egypt, he was not allowed to enter the Promised Land; but it was not just Moses who could not enter. None of the people entered the Promised Land unless they were children or the youngest. Moses got a bad rap. All of the people had become too soft and dependent. The people had to be toughened, disciplined, and strengthened by forty years of hard living in the desert before they could fight their way into their promised land. They had to be trained and prepared for independence, self reliance, and governing themselves in a land of their own, Lincoln knew the slaves would need help, time, and preparation for independence and self-reliance after emancipation. Lincoln tried to make reconstruction a time for healing and lifting before he was assassinated. The second civil war made the existential circumstances of former slaves more difficult, but, against great odds, many former slaves were able to "possess the promised land" in much less time than forty years—but too many are still on the outside looking in. There is now a generation of people in the USA that could be experiencing a period of testing and tough times; and I hope they are not too soft to pass the test. Dramatic changes that make us tougher and more disciplined may be the only way we can get out of the current morass.

People who retire early in life from a regular job or profession but continue doing work that is productive and challenging will, as a general rule, live longer and get more enjoyment and satisfaction out of their remaining years than those who do not. Working conditions on plantations and in Pennsylvania coal mines could accurately be described as awful, but that did not prevent some plantation slaves and coal miners from doing the best they could to be self supporting by accomplishing hard undesirable work. It meant something to their character and self worth partly because it was so hard. Have we become soft; a spoiled and effete nation?

Perhaps; we need more toughness than sensitivity training. We don't need more anger management classes; we need more effective anger aimed with a wise mind and good direction finder. We don't need sympathy and understanding as much as we need a supportive thumbs-up smile or a hard kick in the ass. We don't need summer camps for young people with parties, lazy sunning, and cocktails; we need boot camps for young people with marine drill sergeants. We don't need group therapy; we need group discipline. We don't need political correctness; we need political common sense. We don't need affirmative action by the government; we need affirmative action by the people. We don't need to be more racially sensitive; we need to be more racially blind. We don't need more African-American or Hispanic studies; we need more "how we are all Americans" studies.

We don't need any part of any war unless we go into a war to win and do whatever is necessary to win. Our people don't need pity; we need opportunities, initiatives, and real accomplishments. Our kids don't need "time out" for discipline; they need lots of love and one or two good butt spankings at the right time and for the right reasons and that will be all the spankings they ever need. Fathers should never spank or strike their daughters at any age. Our kids do not need to be reasoned with as much as they need "yes" or "no" without explanations and frequent fun talks. They need to hear strong voices with authority that teaches respect for proper authority. We don't need to be friends with ass holes; we only need to love people who will not defile the most precious thing that we have to offer; our love. We don't need justice for victims as much as we need victims to stand tall and reject a victim identity. We don't need justice for rapists; we need to separate the rapist from his testicles and put him to work to pay restitution. We don't need jails for thieves; we need work camps where they can earn their keep. We don't need to blur the distinction between masculine and feminine; we need to be proud and feel secure in our gender. We do not need more policemen chasing young black men; we need more policemen fraternizing with and mentoring young black men who are underprivileged and fatherless. We need to put paddles back in the hands of elementary school principals.

Most of us develop our perceptions of work early in life and learn from our parents' perceptions of their work. Many parents excel in training their children to hate work by their own disdain of work and fussing about who takes out the trash. The child that grows up perceiving menial work as something his parents have to make him do will learn how to despise menial work; menial work that may be necessary as a first step toward higher paying work. The child who develops a good attitude toward all work has a bright future. The parents must pride school work as the child's most important work; and not make a fuss about who takes out the trash. School work must belong to the child and be his accomplishment; not the parents. The child's success or failure must be his; not the parents. Tell the child he has earned the right to be proud of himself more often than you are proud of him.

Honest work and genuine achievements are the best therapy in the world for low self-esteem and the best creator of good self-esteem. All of us know that unwanted unemployment can harm a man in more ways than simply taking away his job and paycheck. Freud was right when he said that if a person can work well it is the best sign of good mental health. We know that bad things happen to the mind and heart of a person who has no employment and has to endure unwanted idleness. Long term unemployment can rob a man of his will to work. Thomas Carlyle said:

Blessed is he who has found his work; let him ask no other blessedness. He has a work, a life purpose; he has found it, and will follow it. The only happiness a brave man ever troubled himself with asking much about was happiness enough to get his work done. Whatsoever of morality and intelligence; what of patience, perseverance, faithfulness of method, insight, ingenuity, energy; in a word, whatsoever of strength the man had in him will lie written in the work he does. To work; why? It is to try himself against Nature and her everlasting, unerring laws; these will tell a true verdict as to the man.

CHAPTER ELEVEN

THE WORD VERSUS FORCE

Jesus put Christians in a hell of a quandary. According to the Bible, Christ gave them some commandments that sound strange to most of us. Turn the other cheek. Blessed are the meek. Do not resist anyone who is evil. If someone sues you for your coat, let him have your coat and your cloak. Love your enemies. All of these admonitions sound like they are telling Christians to be meek and passive. It was good advice then but is not necessarily always so.

Philosopher Nietzsche mocked Christians when he told them they thought they were virtuous because they had "lame paws." He believed that teachings in scriptures were illogical, irrational, and foolish. He believed they were contrary to the demands of the laws of nature. Doesn't natural evolution require competition to select the fittest for survival? Is a true Christian required to let an enemy harm him or someone he loves without trying to resist and prevent it? Is a Christian supposed to offer his hand to someone that he knows will cut off his arm? Nietzsche is right in some respects; isn't he? Does that mean that Christ was giving bad advice to Christians? Not necessarily.

I have watched Christian preachers squirm when they were trying to explain Christ's commands to love their enemies and turn the other cheek. It is not easy to reconcile those teachings with what we see and practice every day in the world that we live in. Perhaps Christ was telling Christians that if a Roman soldier with a sword in his hand slaps you on the cheek, don't be a damned fool; turn the other cheek or he will cut off your head. Now, that would be rational and make good sense. Another explanation might be that Christ intentionally used startling words and vivid images to try to combat Jewish people's eagerness for a dumb military revolution. He tried to tell his people that his Kingdom would not employ military force or coercion to increase its membership. His Kingdom would rely on another kind of power. History tells us that an awful lot of Christians have not paid much attention to Christ's admonitions and have used all kinds of force, including military force, to increase their numbers and power; including political power. Lincoln ignored the advice of Christ when he decided to use force by waging war even though there was no threat of force being used against the Union. Was Lincoln right to use force? Almost everyone believes he was right but a few historians argue that there was a way to keep the Union together and emancipate slaves without sending masses of men to horrible deaths? We did not ignore Christ when we used force to defend ourselves after Pearl Harbor.

The use of force is ensconced in every law of every government. Stipulated punishments are included in laws. They warn citizens to obey the law; or else! There would be no need for force, or even laws, if everyone willingly and voluntarily did what wise laws command; but that will never happen because there will always be some bad people. Laws are made necessary by bad, not good, behavior. In Utopia, property could be divided and arguments settled by simple agreements and a hand shake but human nature makes Utopia impossible and the most devout Libertarian knows the rule of law and some law enforcement will always be necessary for a good government. Sad to say, I guess lawyers will also always be necessary. However, I think you will agree that free and voluntary good behavior will always be superior to forced behavior.

Force was necessary, and it was good, when it stopped Hitler. It was good when my father whipped me for swimming in a snake infested pond; I never did it again. Force is good when it puts a man in prison for killing one of our policemen. It is good when it protects children and everyone possible from criminal behaviors. It is good when it makes us pay wise, good, and necessary taxes to governments.

I said human nature will always make Utopia impossible but I did not mean to indict human nature as intrinsically evil; even though some think it is. John Locke disputes the existence of instinctual behavior in humans, but most of us now agree that humans still have instincts and manifest innate behaviors. All normal people experience sexual desire, hunger, curiosity, and an urge to make things happen. I define aggression as the desire and efforts to make things happen (good or bad) and I define passivity as the impulse to not resist and to let things happen. Both can be good or bad. All of our incipient emotions and behaviors reside in a reservoir that we call human nature and they become good or bad when they are expressed in behaviors; including expressions of anger, hate, fear, possessiveness, nurturing, bonding, protectiveness, love, and so on. Innate impulses and drives become good or bad only when manifested in human behaviors. This usually occurs when humans interact with and respond to their environment.

We go to a football game and someone yells: "Wow! Look at the size of that linebacker. I hope he flattens that damned quarterback for good on this play." We want our team to be aggressive and dominate the other team with overpowering force on the football field. It is civilized, enjoyable and ritualized pure aggression and fans pay money to watch it. The players love it. The fans enjoy it and vicariously satisfy their aggression by watching it. Football can be brutal but it is more civilized than gladiators fighting in the Roman Coliseum. Civilized countries learn how to ritualize and channel their aggression into competition with limits on the use of force and with fair rules and fair play.

I do not consider war civilized behavior but most great civilizations and Empires were created by wars of conquest. Lincoln preserved the United States of America with war and it may have been the only way that it could have been accomplished; or it may not have been the only way. If a war is not civilized behavior, how can anyone justify war? The most obvious justification is to make it the lesser of two evils. I believe it is just to fight and die for honor, freedom, defense of our home and land, and the protection of people we love. Was the American Civil War the lesser of two evils when there were no other options? I know what almost everyone's verdict is. I wish I could be convinced.

Gandhi, Mandela, Jesus, and Martin Luther King rejected using physical or military force to effect change and relieve social injustice. They used the powers of peaceful protest, reasoning, persuasion, appeals to justice and compassion in men, and manifestations of love and good-will in their behavior. They prevailed and succeeded without resorting to force. They were aggressive in a passive way. They demonstrated the power of persuasion and good-will and proved their power was stronger than a sword. They did not have a sword and we can only trust they would not use it if they had it. In the beginning was the Word and the Word was Love. Do we believe that?

Gandhi obtained independence for India and Mandela for South Africa; Jesus established a new kind of Kingdom; and Reverend King was the most influential person in abolishing the oppressive laws of forced segregation. Perhaps these men were anomalies. Perhaps their successes were exceptions to the rule. Perhaps they were wrong and men like Machiavelli and Napoleon were right. Perhaps it really is better to be feared than loved. Perhaps force applied by any means (lying, dissembling, and killing) is justified by the desired end. I hope that is not true.

After the first war, black people were free in their legal status but still constrained by segregation and their need to work, make a living, and have a place to stay and live in. Few were in a position to bargain about wages. Some black people had good relationships with their former masters and wanted to stay where they were; others may have believed they had no other choice.

When the last Union troops went home (twelve years after Appomattox), segregation did not prevent most black people from freely remaining in the South (see the 1960 and 1970 censuses that I provide). For most black people the only available work was still on plantations.

Machiavelli is an example of strong advocates for military force and using any means to obtain a desired end. He was convinced that the strong must always rule and military force provides the most strength; men must be ruled by the sword. He finds validation of his philosophy in natural law. Survival depends on competition and the fittest (which in his mind were the strongest) always win. Men and baboons are much alike, he thought, and he is right. And, if there is no difference between humans and baboons his philosophy is correct. The laws of nature will always select the fittest for survival by decisive competition; but human beings now define fitness in different ways. A society of baboons is ruled by an oligarchy of a few merciless male thugs. In their society it pays to be a powerful merciless thug. Alpha males accept responsibility for their position and will be the first to fight any predator to protect their troop and alphas make sure the young are protected by keeping them in the safest place; the center of the troop. However, any female caught having sex with a subordinate male is in big painful trouble and the guilty subordinate male is in bigger trouble.

Machiavelli could also find justification for lying and cheating in nature. A female swallow, like a number of other birds, will choose a mate that is not a "hunk" but will be a good provider. Meanwhile other male swallows, that are "hunks", fly around advertising their charms. When the female is ready for sex she will, often, cheat on her husband with a "hunk." Her instinctual reason for cheating is that she wants her male offspring to have the genes of a "hunk" mixed with hers. She wants her male babies to be "hunks" so they are good at seducing females and reproducing his and her genes in another generation of swallows. How does the good provider have his genes reproduced? He often doesn't; but nature "knows" that some of the lady swallow's boys must be born good providers for the specie to survive; and all swallow wives are not unfaithful. (Do some females settle for good provider husbands? Do some cheating wives also copulate with their husband? The ladies will not tell us.)

The dove and the serpent compete by any means possible to reproduce, survive, and thrive. Machiavelli wonders why we should think that humans are different. Machiavelli wonders how anyone can be stupid enough to believe humans are not subject to natural laws and he is right about that; we are not exempt from natural laws. Doesn't might make right? Humans have unique ideas about might; as they do about fitness. Nature has other ways for species to reproduce and survive and some of them are devious.

The lily uses seductive beauty for sex, as does the male peacock and male sage grouse. The poor male praying mantis must rely on stealth because he knows that, if the odorous lady sees him sneaking up from the rear, she will have him for dinner while he is having her for sex. Machiavelli is correct about one thing; we are not exempt from natural laws. Humans are subject to laws of nature and meekness, conciliation, and compromise seem foolish in an uncaring and indifferent world. If we do live in that kind of world then winner-take-all competition is all that matters. However humans learned that there are different kinds of fitness and discovered the fitness of broad cooperation and expansive goodwill much more than any other species. If we live in a caring world we can learn that win-win competition and cooperation with other social groups is our best hope for survival.

The extent and quality of love is a potential unique to humans. The highest love is not innate; it must be acquired from another person; hopefully from many other people. Humans have the potential of becoming friendly, cooperative, loving, reasonable, and astonishingly intelligent—to a level and degree that no other living creature has reached? The Old Testament story of Jonah tells us that men who are motivated by good-will can learn how to extend good-will to people who are outside of their immediate social group—even to nations who are much different in many ways from us. However, the unbridled side of human nature rebels against such a dumb idea as embracing and having friendly, cooperative relationships with people who are much different from us.

It is a fact that men are, by nature, acquisitive, pugnacious, and aggressive but those qualities do not always produce bad behavior. They can be channeled into the service of cooperation, friendship, and love. Only humans will fight to protect a person that he does not know. The fountain of human nature can flow with a river of acceptance or rejection; love or hate; good or ill will. Humans, like all other social species, naturally prefer the company of people and social groups who are the most like them. This instinct, however, can produce prejudice and racism. We need knowledge and understanding to know if other people want to harm us or be our friends. It is <u>not</u> prejudice to avoid the company of someone that we know for a fact wants to hurt us. It <u>is</u> prejudice to make an unfounded erroneous assumption that people we know almost nothing about, want to hurt us.

The reason why Confederate leaders wanted to separate from the Union was <u>not</u> because they did not want to be friends with, trade with, and cooperate with the Union in free and voluntary relationships. They believed the Union was harming them and would continue harming them if they remained in the Union. Human nature produced a blood bath. Does it matter now if States had a constitutional right to secede or the Union had a constitutional right to invade the South and force them back into the Union? I can only hope that someday the South will not be accused as the sole cause of the war.

We have fought other wars that many people believe were a mistake. The war with England, that President Madison wanted and started, was folly. Most of us believe that Viet Nam was a political blunder and a horrible unnecessary war. Many of us believe that it was a bad choice to become involved in land wars in Iraq, Afghanistan, and other nations. Most people in the USA did not want to get into the actual fighting in World War I, but Woodrow Wilson used deceitful tactics and got us in it against the will of the majority. Some of our Presidents waged war without the consent of Congress or the people.

History will determine if force is the strongest power and prevails? I hope the Word will prevail. The powers of personality, ideas, speech, music, the pen, friendship, and loyalty can be arrayed against force. Buddhists, Jews, and Christian tell us about a certain kind of "love" and tell us that its power excels all other powers. For the sake of the human species, I hope they are right. What is unique about that certain kind of love?

It is not "Eros". Eros is essential to survival. Without sex and reproduction we will all soon be history. The powerful instinct bedevils, bewitches and drives men to behave in sane and insane behaviors. It makes some people neurotic and gives other people creative energy. Fathers worry that their daughters will do it too soon and that their sons will do it too late.

Sigmund was correct,
It's all about sex.
Without it man would not exist,
And there's nothing better,
In a sensual way
To give you pleasure.
The elixir of life must hold its sway.
Doves do it, deer do it,
Monkeys up in a tree do it;
People do it and call it love.

Eros wields an awesome power.
It makes the males of many species,
Ignore all perils and bloody dangers.
The girl they desire is all they see.
With fangs and claws and locking horns;
Males battle for her favor.
Men run and fight for a champion's crown.
While women cheer; and vie for winners.

When the God of creation
Gave Eros to nature,
He gave us pleasure with purpose majestic?
Sexes must come together in a touch erotic?
There's no other way for life to flourish;
No other way to obey nature's wish.
Do it like an angel or do it like a beast;
Drink the wine of Eros or cease to exist.

Bob

The power of the instinct is worshiped and feared. Old men lose it; young men misuse it. It can become as misdirected as the automobile of a drunken man. It is hard to think of anything that makes us behave more foolishly. It needs a steady steering wheel and firm brakes to be safe. It needs a sound mind in control of our sexual organs; rather than vice versa.

The unique love is also not just friendship. Mix fondness and friendship with Eros and you get romance. Romance is a dangerous volatile potion.

Ah romance;

So sweet; so bitter.

Nothing else can lift us as high

And sink us as low.

Nothing else can so move us to cry

And cling so hard to a fragile bough

Of emotions; thrilling and overwhelming.

Nothing else can enslave us and mesmerize

With ecstasy and dreams of possessing

The one we adore and idolize.

No other thrill or pleasure can match

A tender embrace in your lover's arms.

No other loss or pain can tear

Your heart into so many pieces,

And shroud your life with bleak despair

As the loss of a love you held so dear.

Ah romance!

It makes old men fools and young men crazy.

It can feel so good and hurt so bad,

But I think it's here to stay.

And I'm glad.

Bob

The unique Love is considered synonymous with God by religions. Greeks called it Agape. It gives and accepts for itself. It needs no other reason. It is expressed by loving acts; loving ourselves and loving others. It is a desire to help and lift that is stronger than the impulse to harm. We hurt people we love; but we always regret it. Our motives are often mixed, conflicted, and confusing but we can know if love is our ruling desire and we fall below our true self when we hurt someone we love. It can excel all other wishes but it cannot erase, or extinguish, the existence of base motives in human nature.

Here is a description of how Agape works that was written many decades ago by Professor William Hyde in *Five Great Philosophies*:

> (Agape) does not judge us by the formal test of whether we have kept or broken this or that specific commandment, but by the deeper and more searching requirement that our lives shall detract nothing from and add something to the glory of God and the welfare of man.
>
> Is this world a happier, holier, better world because we are here in it, helping on God's goodwill for men? If that be the grand, comprehensive purpose of our lives, honestly cherished, frankly avowed, systematically cultivated, then, no matter how far below perfection we may fall, that single purpose, in spite of failure, defeat, and repented sin, pulls us through.

Agape does not transform life into a "piece of cake" but it can help us get through the worst of times. Negative emotions can drag us down and but these times are exceptions and not the rule. We can know if our predominant behavior is motivated by a unique Love.

Agape instructs us in the wisdom of the best behavior for ourselves and others. It is the sails and rudder of good and wise competition and cooperation. It does not abolish law; it fulfills law. When love rules, the best that man can hope for is here and now. Law is written in the heart and all that a good law requires becomes what we most desire and freely follow. Force, coercion, and seduction can be cast away like a broken cup.

Is all of this nothing more than the muttering and superstitious fantasy of an old man, or can that kind of love actually work in real life? Was it in the mind and heart of Lincoln? What if Lincoln had bid the seceded States "good-bye and good luck"? Could the seceded States return and freely join all other States in a better Union? Could emancipation be accomplished with willing handshakes and the mutual best interests of the races?

CHAPTER TWELVE

DUELING GOVERNMENTS

"The Tea Party can go straight to hell" said Congresswoman Maxine Waters. Some members of the Black Caucus display down-right unfriendly feelings toward conservative groups that push for a smaller Government. Waters thinks the government needs to do more rather than less. It is not a new argument; in fact, it is older than our Constitution. The difference now between Democrats and Republicans is about the size and functions of government. Hamilton and Jefferson had the same argument; a strong Central Government that rules the States or a weak limited Central Government with State and individual sovereignty carefully protected in a Constitution. Hamilton's idea prevailed in 1851. Our present Government is a legacy of two civil wars.

All modern governments can be found somewhere on a spectrum between two extremes. On one end is the strong authoritarian Dictatorship. On the other end is a Libertarian and limited Central Government with preeminent powers in State and local Governments, and abundant individual freedoms. Let me use extremes to make a sharp contrast between them and different characteristics of the majority in their populations. Remember, these are extremes to a point of foolishness.

Here is one view; the extreme Libertarian and some conservatives' view. Almost everyone is trustworthy and responsible with a small need for laws. Therefore, the whole nation is rosy and prosperous. All of my stocks are going up and the economy couldn't be better. All of our kids are becoming better educated and better citizens with good jobs waiting when they finish school. I have complete personal freedom and civil liberties. Social relationships are splendid. My wife let me out of the doghouse and gave me a kiss. My teenage daughter actually smiled at me. My boss gave me a raise and I got young, rich, and handsome in my dreams last night. There are no goons, crooks, or lunatics with larceny, rape, or murder on

111

their mind anywhere. No one in the nation lies, cheats, steals, assaults, rapes, or seduces another man's wife. Everyone is as free as the wind and as far removed from harm as I am from playing professional football. (The Sunday school teacher asked a little boy what we must do before we can be forgiven and the little boy answered "sin.") No one needs forgiveness or laws in our perfect nation because we have no faults. No one needs protection or policemen. Coercion, force, intimidation, and seduction are as nonexistent as fleas on my well groomed and pampered cocker spaniel. Love and goodness reign universally supreme. Everyone is benevolent, friendly, honest, trustworthy, and self reliant. Our government is small, weak, and trusts all citizens to govern themselves wisely and we like it.

That sounds like a dream world because that is exactly what it is. There are no perfect nations because there are no perfect people. There is no common good without relinquishing some individual freedoms.

What is the opposite view? The people must be sternly ruled because they cannot be trusted and are irresponsible. Going to hell in a basket? No! We are already in hell. The nation is as decadent as a Roman bacchanalia. Special interests control all of our money. All politicians are compromised, greedy, liars, and don't give a damn about anything but getting elected and reelected. We are bankrupt and going down the tubes faster than an out of control snow skier. Hedonism rules our culture and Rappers are now our philosophers. Everyone is selfish, irresponsible, untrustworthy, and needs to be controlled like little children. No one cares about anyone but himself. (Two men were running from a bear. One said: "It's no use; we will never outrun that bear." The other said: "I don't have to outrun the bear; all that I have to do is outrun you.") Our philosophy is let the devil take the hindmost. Root hog or die. No one gives a damn about me and I don't give a damn about you. Our situation is dire. We must have a big strong government to save us. We need a dictator and an army of policemen.

Our nation swings back and forth like a pendulum on a continuum of opposite extremes in our politics and perceptions. The overall trend, since 1861, is toward a strong authoritarian Central Government. We could be ready to swing in the opposite direction. The pendulum can swing fast or slow. With our amazing technology and instant worldwide communication, drastic cultural change can now occur in an eye blink.

Do voters determine the swing? The most common character of the people determines the character and type of the elected government;

unless candidates are persuasive liars. Is this statement accurate; the more trustworthy the people are, the less government is needed? Is this statement accurate; the more untrustworthy people are; the more we need a strong authoritarian central government? Let me ask one more question. Can government make people more trustworthy or less trustworthy? I believe the answer is "yes" to all of the questions. The perceptions of most common citizens by leaders make a difference. Leaders with a low opinion of citizens want more authority; leaders with a high opinion of citizens want less authority. Do all of these ideas go into the thinking of voters? Both the intelligence level and the emotions of people determine their vote. Socrates and men before him debated the value of intelligence versus emotions in voters in the choice of government. Hamilton believed that voters should meet high standards of knowledge, literacy, and intelligence to qualify as a voter.

Can government and social programs save the nation? Historian Will Durant said: "He (Christ) resembled Caesar only in taking his stand with lower classes, and in the quality of mercy; otherwise what a world of outlook, character, and interests separated them! Caesar hoped to reform men by changing institutions and laws; Christ wished to remake institutions, and lessen laws, by changing men." Behavioral psychologists and Dictators disagree most unpleasantly with Christ on this point.

Both Conservatives and Liberals like some teachings of Christ. Conservative like what Christ said about government, economics, and reality when he defended property rights. He told the story of a worker who grumbled because an employer paid a man who worked only one hour as much as the employer paid him for working all day. The employer said: "Is it not lawful for me to do what I will with my own?" Jesus gives the employer a right to his property and the right to use it as he chooses.

Christ taught lessons about reality. A master went on a journey and left money in the care of three slaves. The slave that had ten minas invested and doubled the money. The slave that had one mina played it safe and did not invest it. When the master returned he praised the slave that invested and doubled his money and scolded the unproductive slave. Christ spoke hard words: "To him who has, more will be given, and from him who has nothing, even that which he has will be taken away." Sounds harsh, doesn't it? But its reality isn't it? The market place is what it is and life is what it is. It is a stern practical lesson that life is sometimes unfair but that is how we must take it when it is unchangeable reality. Risk takers are people who make and lose a lot of money. Money under a mattress will only lose value by inflation. Early Christianity was risky if a Christian did not hide his religion; he could become lion food. Complaining and becoming resentful does nothing to change reality. Sometimes life smells like honey and sometimes it stinks.

Christ did not condemn interest earned by investing or lending even though interest was condemned by Jewish law. He did not condemn or condone slavery; he took established institutions for granted. Jesus did not foresee an end to poverty; "The poor you have always with you."

Liberals like what Christ said when he gave the rich hell; literally and figuratively; and praised the poor and the Good Samaritan for helping a person in trouble. It is a fact that riches and power corrupt many, perhaps most, people and it is harder to change that reality than it is for a camel to go through the eye of a needle. "Sell your property, give your money to the poor, and . . . follow me." Christ did not criticize the government. Render unto Caesar that which is Caesar's; pay your taxes and don't bitch about it. A poor man looked down at a rich man burning in hell, begging for water; the poor man would not, or could not, give him a drop. Rich men build their houses on sand and lose everything in a storm. The early Christians lived in a communist community which "had all things in common." When people were hungry, Christ fed them by miraculously multiplying a few fishes and loaves of bread into enough food for everyone. When people were sick, Christ touched and healed them. Repent you wicked rich sinners because the judgment day is right around the corner.

Christ advised the motley little band that followed him that it would be a mistake to attempt a military revolution. Accept reality; the Romans are much stronger and would crush you; and they did. Don't cause trouble. Be meek and passive. Turn the other check. We cannot win a rebellion against the Roman government. Obey the laws and pay your taxes.

Turning the other check was good advice, but had nothing to do with morality; it would not make Christians virtuous. It was a warning. Jews wanted to try to overthrow the Roman government with a militant uprising and Christ said don't try it. They tried anyway and the Diaspora soon scattered them to many distant lands. When Christ did not sound a call to arms and instead, advocated a meek, submissive, and non-violent response to Roman rule, the long suffering and oppressed Jews were angry and sorely disappointed. It was wisdom, not cowardice, to turn the other cheek. (If a sword was on my neck, I would turn my cheek as many times as the soldier wanted and I may give him a few extra turns for good measure. I may even try to make him think that I loved him but, inside, I would hate his guts and not feel the least bit guilty if I could turn the table and have my sword at his neck.)

Christ brought a revolution but not the kind of revolution his people wanted. His revolution would be accomplished by power but not by force. Let me repeat; accomplished by power and not force. The most common description of that power is that it is spiritual. The Christian religion has used the force of the sword many times in wars to conquer and to persecute and to enforce doctrines, and all such uses of force rejected Christ's admonitions.

Someone said that all of our tomorrows will be more alike than different from our yesterdays. As human beings, people in 1851 were much the same as people today. We have more knowledge today and may be a bit more civilized. Did our first civil war change men? It accomplished drastic governmental change in the relatively short span of four years. Did it make us better persons with better behavior and personal relationships? The war changed the government and laws and the legal status of a race of people. The nation was united by compulsion and the central government garnered much greater power and authority. Did this make our government and our people better? Did it eliminate racism and prejudice? I believe time and knowledge has reduced prejudice. I believe Cesar would applaud our civil war. I believe Christ would say there was a better way.

Fareed Zakaria, author of *The Future of Freedom*, comprehensively researched different governments around the world gathering, an immense amount of facts and statistics. He makes a compelling argument that a free and open democracy requires at least three things and one of them is a large bourgeoisie class. By bourgeoisie, he means "ambitious, aggressive small capitalists—industrious property-owning class—the owners of the means of production of a society and employer of its laborers." Without a large class of producers that employ workers, a sustainable open democracy is economically impossible. He describes some democracies that are cruel and intolerant. Many open and free democracies had to evolve step by step and stage by stage in a way that prepared them for a free democracy. The quality of a good government is sustained only by the good quality of its people. Remember Jeremiah? How well were our slaves prepared for freedom?

Kakaria describes how China has slowly but steadily been making its nation more open, tolerant, and modern. The Communist Party still rules China with an iron hand but they have been making economic and social reforms since 1980 and, in some places, allowing local democratic type elections. They are gradually reducing State control of factories, industry, private businesses, and commercial enterprises. They have been carrying out land reforms as well as economic reforms and accepting an emergence of capitalism. He writes: "The economic results of China's reforms have been staggering. Between 1980 and 2000 the average person's income in China almost tripled, from $1,394 to $3,976. Some 170 million people have moved above the poverty line. Their gradual changes are slowly preparing the people for a democracy and heading in the direction of an open tolerant democracy. They have been balancing economic and social liberalization with political control. "If (a big "if") China continues on its current path and continues to grow, further develops its rule of law, builds a bourgeois, and then liberalizes its politics it will have achieved an extraordinary transformation toward genuine democracy." The road they are traveling will most likely end in democracy or riots and rebellion. If freedom and democracy comes to China, the people will be prepared for it. (Russia has followed the opposite path of sudden and drastic overthrows of the government and their economy has been in shambles—saved to some extent by the rise in oil prices.)

The economic and social conditions of the black race might be better today if we used the methods of Christ rather than those of Cesar in the 1800s. The plantation slaves could have been prepared for the path to freedom and self reliance with time, and the best kind of help. That would have been in the best self-interests of everyone. Jefferson Davis essentially gave his slaves the choice of returning or not returning when they went on trips. The fundamental sectional conflicts of interests in 1851were economic and political; slavery was involved only because their votes could determine political power.

CHAPTER THIRTEEN

PROS AND CONS

Bipedal apes with big brains, that we call humans, provide the sails and rudder for our Ship of State and the apes, much too often, steer like drunken sailors. The majority is not always right but they are supposed to possess decisive power in our democracy Past majorities have chosen markedly different kinds of leaders and governments. Exceptionally strong leaders can take a nation wherever they want it to go; with or without the majority of the people. When the people choose their form of government, their choice does not guarantee a correct course, even though their nation is a Democracy.

All humans are flawed; some more, and some (like me) less flawed than others. All humans are good *and* bad. The character and behaviors of some individuals and groups tip the scale on the side of goodness; and vice versa. That is an essential distinction between different governments and the norm of their people. All men (notice, that to escape female fury, I am excluding women) are by nature pugnacious, acquisitive, competitive, and get enjoyably excited when a fist fight breaks out in a hockey game. However, everyone but sadists will feel bad if a player on either team is seriously injured. Innate aggression and natural conflicts of interests will always instigate conflicts and wars. Some Libertarians will not accept that reality. They sometimes try to deny the reality of evil nations with our blood in their eyes.

One side of human nature can be as dark as a moonless night without street lights; another side can be as bright as new snow in sunlight. Robert Ardrey, a brilliant student of man and nature, describes us like this: "Classic is our daring, classic is our cowardice. Classic is our cruelty, classic our charity. No human inventory can fail to include our propensity for premeditated, organized murder of our fellows yet fail to note that an army is a model of cooperation and self-sacrifice, or that no other species so carefully, tenderly cares for its wounded, even for its enemies. Compassion and mercy lies deep in our nature, as deep perhaps as our callousness and indifference."

Why is human nature flawed and governments' necessary? Blame all of it on Eve again. Eve, the Good Book tells us, was so damned hard-headed and inquisitive that she insisted on tasting the apple. She was overwhelmed with curiosity and a desire to know. She wanted to discover what would happen if she ate that apple. She was told that it would give her knowledge and wisdom. She wanted to find out for herself. Was she curious and reckless because she was human or did curiosity make her human? She must have had a powerful need to know. When humans acquired choices they acquired choices of good and bad expressions of their innate impulses, instincts, and drives. God gave Eve choice. Eve made the choice for knowledge and all of the baggage that comes with it. When she tasted the apple; good and evil became a reality and the human conscience was born.

Isn't that just like a woman? My wife wants to know everything that is going on in the neighborhood; and she has a way of finding out. The only thing I know is what she tells me. Eve must have been as inquisitive and stubborn as a two year old. Why did Eve have to eat that apple? She got herself into a heap of trouble; and Adam too. This fall (and rise) of Eve is what St. Augustine called the original sin that makes all of us born sinners. Eve probably was a sinner, like you and me, but, to me, Eve was also a heroine. She took a risk to make a choice. She wanted knowledge and paid the price to obtain it. Put two and two together. Without human knowledge and choice, we would have no civilization. Without Eve we would have no knowledge. Knowledge (alias Eve) made civilization possible. That is why she is a heroine to me. Eve chose knowledge and wisdom over ignorance and innocence. However, Rousseau said civilization is not that great; it robs innocence and produces tons of guilt.

Why do we call Eve a sinner? The story in Genesis can be confusing. God told Adam (and presumably Eve) that he would die if he ate fruit from the tree that would give him knowledge of good and evil. Adam ate the fruit and did not die—unless God meant that disobedience would make him human and subject to death. The serpent told Eve that she would not die if she ate the fruit and she ate the fruit and did not die. Whatever the meaning of the story, it is a remarkable description of how we became humans. We developed the evolutionary critical human pair bond—even though my wife doesn't buy the part about me ruling over here. We developed cerebral knowledge and wisdom that could be passed down from generation to generation and become towers filled with transmittable knowledge.

The story in Genesis has a factual history of how civilization began. It is almost miraculous foresight. We learned how to till the soil, domesticate animals, and stay in one place long enough to develop villages and unifying cultures. Eventually villages united and created city states and so on until we created civilizations with governments. However, knowledge, civilizations and governments come with a price. They come with choices and consequences; benefits and liabilities.

It is trite but true; no civilization or government can ever be a Garden of Eden. Shit happens and always will. All of us go through trials of pain, sorrow, tough times, and the grief of a loved one's death. In some places, life can be extremely hard. Before he became the Buddha, Siddhartha, a rich man's son, left his wife and child to escape the harsh realities of existence in a world marred by illness, woes, and death. He became a bum and beggar. (I wonder what his wife thought of her husband becoming a bum. One way to avoid being corrupted by wealth is to not get wealthy. My wife may wish for a little more money and corruption from me.) Siddhartha became an ascetic and nearly starved himself to death; but that did not work. Eventually, he discovered that he could get into an altered state of consciousness, escape reality, and enjoy the bliss of Nirvana by sitting under a tree and meditating.

Augustine believed our only escape from this cruel life is to die and go to heaven. Rousseau did not blame human nature for the bad things that people did; he blamed society and civilization, "I was born good (innocent) but society made me evil." Socialists and behavioral psychologists jumped on this idea and, with a little twist, said that if society made us evil, society can make us good. "In social programs we place our trust."

We can never live in a Garden of Eden, but we can get close to it with expert meditation, religious experiences, or chemicals. Remember, we have choice and options. We have no choice or control over natural events, such as rain and sunshine, but we have choices of risking or playing it safe.

I don't think many of us want to follow Rousseau and return to the jungle and live on leaves and termites; but he is right in a way, and wrong in a way, isn't he? He was right when he said society is flawed, unjust, unequal, and unfair. Look at the crooks in society. He was wrong when he said society makes people evil and socialists are wrong when they say that society can cure all ills. Human nature contains the seeds of good and bad behavior and the choices we make of behaviors have good and bad consequences. There is no one responsible for your choices and their consequences but you; if you are old enough to be responsible for yourself. Society, especially family, can make good choices and behavior easier or harder, but society cannot make our choices for us. When human beings choose freedom in their lives they make themselves responsible for their freedom.

Government can relieve us from responsibility by making choices for us and subtracting from our freedom. This means that the kind of government we want is directly related to how much freedom we choose and how much responsibility we are willing to accept. The fact that we have a strong authoritarian Government speaks volumes about the people in the USA. We lost our innocence in Eden but gained the possibility of becoming free and human, but it depends on us. Bad people will always cause serious problems. An over abundance of bad people will always produce oppressive governments. In the long run, people and the government go up or down together. Freedom can be a curse or a blessing and is not for weak or irresponsible people.

Where did all of our liberty and freedom go? Many people are exchanging freedom for a pot of porridge. Many other people are fighting the excessive controls of laws and governments for more freedoms. Adam and Eve were never ashamed of being naked or up-tight about sex before they got the pair-bond, big brain, laws, religion, society, government, and, most of all, choices granted to no other creature. O, for the good old days. I think I will go to a nudist camp so that I can experience the freedom of a naked native for a little while—if my wife will go with me. I am too chicken to go without her. Or maybe I will go to Woodstock and smoke some pot. Hateful rules and restrictions of civilization can be such a bore and so depressing. Now I know why teen-age boys and girls (and sixty year old men who are in their second childhood; or never grow out of adolescence) rebel against rules, their parents, and the establishment. The laws of Moses are a drag. They crimp my freedom and Moses thought they were necessary just because some stupid sex addicts were worshiping a golden calf. Wait for me Rousseau, I'm coming with you.

So, it's plain to see. We can blame Moses and Eve and calf worshipers for all of our problems. The rule of law and jails are necessary because humans do stupid things. Some try to harm people if they are not locked up. We want to be like Adam and Eve. We want knowledge and the freedom to make our own choices like daring Eve. Now our Patriarchal Nanny Government thinks that is wrong. Politicians believe that human beings are much too untrustworthy to think and choose for themselves. The Government must do it for us. Only the Government can make us good; by making more rules, regulations, and laws. I hope the pendulum is ready to swing toward more freedom and less authoritarian governmental control? (I would love to see a moderate Libertarian elected President but that will probably never happen in my lifetime. Many Libertarians are too naïve and unrealistic; especially about foreign policy, but we definitely have too many restrictions and too little liberty. Our Constitution and Bill of Rights are becoming what Hamilton and Madison wanted them to be; "a fragile and worthless piece of fabric.")

I have been describing two fundamentally different philosophies of government. The founding fathers gave us a Constitution and Bill of Rights with the hope and intent of assuring an abundance of liberty and freedom for individuals and States, and a viable and reasonably strong central government with a guarantee that we would never have another King. Hamilton and Madison fought Jefferson. The central argument began during the birth and early years of our nation and they were intense. The argument continues today but many citizens do not clearly understand the argument and the issues at stake. The clear winner of the argument became Hamilton in 1865, with the aid of Lincoln. The dominance of the Central Government has waxed and waned since then but has never been in danger of a serious loss of its authority, power, and control. After the war, Lincoln wanted to restore some authority and rights to the States, but it was not to be.

At some places in some eras, a Dictator is needed. A Dictatorship that works is the most efficient form of government. Germany's remarkable rapid rise of industry, employment, prosperity, and military power under Hitler is a prime example. Dictators are ambitious, aggressive, and never satisfied with how much they control. They overreach and their ambition makes and breaks them. This was not true of Lincoln after the war. Strong central governments require individuals and groups to forfeit civil liberties and freedoms. Freedom cannot reign without integrity, trustworthiness, and responsibility in a large majority of the people. That kind of integrity and responsibility has become as scarce in our nation as the hair on my balding head—but I hope our chances of regaining those qualities are better than my chances of growing more hair. Here are some quotes to illustrate sharp contrasts in philosophies of government; beginning with Libertarians and many Conservatives.

"Government, even in its best state, is but a necessary evil; in its worst state, an intolerable one. Government, like dress, is the badge of lost innocence; the palaces of kings are built upon the ruins of the bowers of paradise." Thomas Paine

"The only purpose for which power can be rightfully exercised over any member of a civilized community, against his will, is to prevent harm to others." (To protect the well defined rights of life, liberty, and property.) John Stuart Mill

"But it would seem that if despotism were to be established amongst the democratic nations of our days, it might assume a different character; it would be more extensive and milder; it would degrade men without tormenting them. I do not question, that in any age of instruction and equality, like our own, sovereigns might more easily succeed in collecting all political power into their own hands, and might interfere more habitually and decidedly within the circle of private interests, than any sovereign of antiquity could ever do."
Alexis de Tocqueville

"The average man, whatever his errors otherwise, at least sees clearly their government is something lying outside him and outside the generality of fellow men—that it is a separate, independent and often hostile power, only partially under his control, and capable of doing him great harm . . . . What lies behind all this, I believe, is a deep sense of the fundamental antagonism between the government and the people it governs. It is apprehended, not as a committee of citizens chosen to carry on the communal business of the whole population, but as a separate and autonomous corporation, mainly devoted to exploiting the population for the benefit of its own members." H. L. Mencken

Some of these men may not identify themselves as Libertarians but they give you the flavor of Libertarians' and many Conservatives' love for freedom and independence; except to smoke pot. Here is a quote from a man with libertarian thinking who acknowledges the essential need for government:

"The existence of a free market does not of course eliminate the need for government. On the contrary, government is essential both as a forum for determining the "rules of the game" and as an umpire to interpret and enforce the rules decided on." Milton Freidman

"The most desirable laws are those which are fewest, simplest and most general. I think moreover that it would be better to have none at all than to have them in the profusion as we do now . . . . When King Ferdinand sent colonies of immigrants to the Indies he made the wise stipulation that no one should be included who had studied jurisprudence, less law suits should pullulate in the New World." Montaigne

Here are some quotes from an extreme advocate for a strong central government. Machiavelli was one of the most radical champions of supreme central power and authority. Unlike Aristotle, who gave us the "Golden Mean" and a wise way to use common sense to judge the wisdom of means by the end they serve, Machiavelli believes that the end he seeks justifies any kind of means and that a strong Ruler should have no concern about the morality, or immorality, of the means he uses to conquer and hold his domain. He was the kind of man that the Constitution and Bill of Rights tried to shield the nation from.

Infamous Machiavelli longed to see the City States of Italy brought into one strong central government and Machiavelli condemns the Church <u>not</u> for protecting her temporal power, but for <u>not</u> using all her resources to bring all of Italy under her political rule.

A nation can never be united and happy except when it obeys only one government, whether a republic or a monarchy, as is the case in

France and Spain; and the one cause why Italy is not in the same condition is the Church. For having acquired and holding a temporal dominion, yet she has never had sufficient power or courage to enable her to seize the rest of the country and make herself the sole sovereign of Italy.

Machiavelli is not thought of as an evil man because he wanted to unify Italy; he is criticized for the tactics that he recommends to all aspiring princes. A sovereign can ignore the moral code of his people. "When the act accuses him the result should excuse him." Any means used are justified by the end. Cruelties and crimes committed in order to preserve one's country are "honorable frauds"; "glorious crimes". Here are more that he said:

> War violates all the commandments of Moses and Jesus by swearing, lying, stealing, and killing by the thousands; nevertheless, if it preserves the society, or strengthens it, it is good. Rebellious despots who need to be subdued are assailable in no other way. A dictator must be capable of murdering by the million to enforce conformity.
>
> Where it is an absolute question of the welfare of our country, we must admit of no considerations of justice or injustice, of mercy or cruelty, of praise or ignominy, but putting all else aside we must adopt whatever course will save the nation's existence and liberty.
>
> Though a prince need not posses all the virtues, to seem to have them is useful; as, for example, to seem merciful, loyal, humane, religious, and sincere; it is also useful to be so, but with a mind so flexible that if the need arise he can be the contrary . . . He should be careful to let nothing fall from his lips that is not instinct with the five qualities mentioned, and must appear to those who see and hear him all compassion, all faith, all humanity, all religion, all integrity . . . One must color his conduct and be a great dissembler; and men are so simple, so absorbed in present necessities, that they are easily deceived . . . everyone sees what you appear to be, few know what you are; <u>and those few dare not oppose the opinion of many.</u>

Is our government too restrictive or too permissive? Does it have an honest intention to restrict itself? Does every bureau and agency resist the natural tendency to expand its powers and domain?

A plethora of laws incubates a plethora of lawyers. Many people now believe that laws and lawyers have a suffocating stranglehold on America. Spill a cup of coffee on yourself in a restaurant and a dozen lawyers will appear before you can leave wanting to sue the restaurant for making the coffee too hot. At one time all lawyers were highly esteemed and would never think of advertising their practice. Fareed Zakaria, in *The Future of Freedom,* tells us how we used to see our lawyers as "watch dogs" but now we see them as "lap dogs". Now, lawyers buy enticing advertisements on television to tell people that they can get a bundle of money by classifying themselves as victims and authorizing old "Strong Arm" to sue old "Deep Pockets". Some people call it blackmail. People who never knew they had a sickness or injury are now convinced that they have one or the other, or both, and can sue a bad doctor, employer, or cooperation for their condition.

An increase in the number of laws will always produce an increase in the number of law breakers and employment for lawyers, regulators, and policemen to enforce the laws—and lawyers to defend the law breakers. In 1910 the city of Waterloo, Nebraska, passed an ordinance that said "It shall be illegal for any barber in this town to eat onions between 7 AM and 7 PM." That law must have created employment for an onion smeller specialist, a policeman to arrest onion eating law breakers, a lawyer to prosecute and a lawyer to defend the onion eater; a lawyer to represent the man who sues the barber claiming that his lung cancer was caused by his barber's onion breath, a lawyer to fight the suit, and a lawyer to represent the barber when he declares bankruptcy after losing the case.

I hope people are catching on to the nonsense of trying to legally micromanage the private personal behavior of people and, I hope, Libertarian ideas are catching the eyes of increasing numbers of people and gaining serious consideration as common sense reforms. Increased numbers of people also see the mistake of a Federal Central Government managing and tying the hands of State and local governments. This is reflected in the chorus of voices calling for a smaller government.

Libertarians love the Epicurean philosophy. The philosophy emphasizes the importance of simple pleasures and freedom from burdensome rules, regulations, and oversized ambitions. Senator Ron Paul is ignoring

Epicurus because Epicurus advises people not to burden themselves by running for high offices. However, the philosophy has a rule. The cardinal rule of Epicurus is "prudence"; not unbridled Hedonism. The same is true of Libertarians. Libertarians trust people to exercise prudence and wisely govern themselves.

Libertarians believe that pleasure and freedoms are good when people exercise prudence in their enjoyment of them; the Nanny government is a kill joy. Our country will be more content if the people relearn how to enjoy the simple pleasures. The modern hypersexual pop culture is like a cup of champagne that is too full and bubbling over. Do they exercise prudence? I will not judge young people because they are a different generation that puzzles me; as the young always puzzle and are criticized by the older generation.

Libertarians do not advocate lawlessness, riotous living, drug addiction, lewd behaviors, immoral living, and greedy and excessive consumptions of food, alcohol, drugs, and sex. Epicurus wrote: "When we say, then, that pleasure is the end and aim, we do not mean the pleasure of the prodigal, or the pleasures of sensuality, as we are understood by some who are either ignorant and prejudiced for other views, or inclined to misinterpret our statements . . . It is not an unbroken succession of drinking feasts and of revelry . . . It is sober reasoning, searching out the reasons for each choice and avoidance, and banishing those beliefs through which great tumults take possession of the soul." Libertarians say: "A men."

Libertarians enlarge the decisive and crucial importance of free, spontaneous, and prudent behavior and the <u>responsibility</u> of making choices. Prudence in the choice and amount of pleasures is the highest value. Libertarians give us a good tonic for the guilt that needlessly spoils harmless pleasures. It rescues pleasure from foolish condemnations by Puritans and self righteous guardians of other people's behaviors (like Bill O'Reilly). It advocates the simple life and simple pleasures. Libertarianism will not give us a Winston Churchill, Albert Einstein, Thomas Edison, John Glen, or Abraham Lincoln but they will always be good medicine for Prince and pauper, Kings and common men, when taken in prudent doses without unrealistic expectations. It can improve lives and relationships and enhance our enjoyment of measured pleasures. In the phrase of my dear Louisiana Cajuns, Libertarians beckon us to "let the good times roll" but make sure that you love and be good to your neighbors and don't act like a damn fool or hurt someone.

If our nation is soft, as the President said, we must be able to endure pain to become tougher. Libertarians must not ignore the reality and potential value and harm of pain. If necessary, we can learn to accept and endure unavoidable pain for the greater good of serenity and peace of mind. The seeds of Libertarianism fall on barren ground in the fields of self-made martyrs, Puritans, and Ascetics. It makes pain normal and intelligible and shields a man in pain from the acid that misguided moralists pour into his wounds; telling him that his pain is God's punishment for his sin. Libertarians expose the sins of religions.

A true Libertarian does not believe that his philosophy can make the world perfect and free from pain and bad behavior; or have no need for governments but Libertarians can free pain and pleasure from the dark shadows of Puritanical condemnation, religious hypocrisy, and an excessively controlling government.

One of the most fundamental behaviors of all living creatures is to avoid pain and seek pleasure. The first impulse of a newborn infant is to cry for relief from pain and cling to mother for comfort. It is a principle that can help us understand and make sense out of hard to understand behaviors—such as the adolescent girl who intentionally burns or cuts herself. That behavior can only be explained as a way of trying to relieve a greater pain; such as the pain of guilt or rejection. She is obeying a fundamental principle of behavior.

Are we supposed to believe that Jesus was always somber, serious, and that he frowned on pleasure? Did he condemn Epicurus? We are told that Jesus was genuinely human and became angry and cried but I never recall a place in the Bible where Jesus laughed; and I do not remember it being included in a sermon. I want to believe that Jesus joked, and laughed, and experienced enjoyment. Jesus did not quickly condemn pleasures like my church did when I was a child. Hide the playing cards; the pastor is coming. Is it sacrilegious to think that Jesus laughed, sang, and enjoyed the company of friends? He wanted the company of little children. Can we let Jesus be truly and fully human without losing faith in him?

Libertarians value freedom more than wealth. People can enjoy living with or without wealth if they have freedom and integrity. They counsel the father who works too hard, injures his health, and ignores his family to amass an unneeded and unnecessary huge portfolio of stocks. They prefer the less complicated life and the simple pleasures that are available to almost everyone and can be had for the asking. This is common sense and a low bar for behavior that makes the failure of so many of us to reach it even more inexcusable.

The glory and pleasures of an after-life was a comforting philosophy for slaves who were trying to make the best they could out of an inescapable situation. But they invented simple pleasures and other compensations. Slaves were human beings like you and I. I believe that many did the best they could to experience some pleasure and enjoyment. Their religion, singing, and music were genuine expressions of themselves; and ways of bolstering their spirit and hope. We have music today that we would not have without the slaves and black people.

Libertarians would never tell a slave or poor person to be glad he is a slave or poor. They would encourage a slave or poor person to change and improve his circumstances if he wants to and can, but, if that is not possible, to find pleasure and enjoyment in simple things. The best measure of a person is not just who far he goes and how high he climbs; the best measure is how well he can overcome burdens and handicaps to make a life for himself and others worth living. A person who stereotypes a class or race of people tells us more about himself than he does about anyone else.

The best government can rely on the free, spontaneous, and responsible behavior of its citizens when they are free and responsible. When the opposite is true, the people need a Despot. When most of the people become too passive and shirk responsibility, they need a despot. When people are too ignorant and uneducated to govern themselves, they need a despot. Lincoln did not go to the people to make his most important decision; his most important counsel was with himself. I wish he would have let the people decide.

The best government employs force and compulsion only when it is clearly necessary and wise. We can gauge how much a government trusts its citizens by the kind and amount of control that the government deems necessary; however, it is natural for governments to want to expand their power and domain regardless of the character of its citizens. It is certainly better for a government to assume that the people are trustworthy and allow people to prove it by governing themselves—unless there is overwhelming factual evidence that the people cannot be trusted.

The Supreme Court could not trust Southern opinions when the South clung too long to forced segregation and the Court was right to act. On the other hand, the Presidents that got us into World War I and the Viet Nam war were wrong when they did not go to the people and let them decide about war. The best government will restrict freedom only when a person wants to harm another person or the nation. The best government does not protect us from ourselves and will not try to shield individuals or social groups from suffering the bad natural consequences of bad or stupid behavior. It does not artificially reward or punish any person. It does not try to engineer certain social outcomes that disregard merit and accomplishments. An excessively authoritarian government displays a strong mistrust of its citizens, and is convinced that government must do their thinking, deciding, and acting for them; much as a parent must do for an infant. I hope that kind of government is not needed in the USA as much as the current Government seems to think that it does

Excessively restrictive governments do not trust free competition. They want to pick and determine the winners and losers. It diminishes the importance of merit and favors patronage. It knows how to pander, when necessary, to stay in power. The best government does not treat people like strict parents of little unruly children who spank their children too much. (My wife puts me in time-out and sends me to husbands' obedience training if I get unruly. I am practicing good behavior right now because I just got off of probation.) Good governments do not use unnecessary coercion and an overactive policeman's baton to rule their citizens.

We have changed the legal status of the black race from slaves to free men but does our government perceive black and white poor people as helpless little children and demean them? The war changed our government from a mostly free country (for white people) into a dictatorship; a dictatorship that was necessary during our first Civil War. Lincoln, like all war presidents and dictators, must have memorized and slept with a copy of Machiavelli's, *The Prince*, under his pillow. After the war, the radicals wanted to establish permanent Federal control of the South, but Lincoln did not want that. In the short and long run, the punitive and excessively authoritarian rule of the radicals during our second Civil War helped no one, white or black, while creating racial and social resentment all over the country. Our government is now, like most governments, ruled by a rich and powerful Oligarchy. Wisely or foolishly, we have moved closer to Machiavelli than Thomas Jefferson.

The word "dependent" should not always be understood as a pejorative. I depend on my wife, and my wife on me, but it is optional, voluntary, and, I believe, matures. The dependency could be excessive and childish and create ambivalence and resentment. Isn't it wonderful to hear about two perfect people in a perfect marriage with never a problem? Dependency and control present problems in all marriages; except ours, of course. Dependency and control presents problems to governments and their people and that constitutes one of nation's fundamental problems.

There is a natural desire in many people to turn their personal responsibility over to a leader who will tell them what to do and make big decision for them. Those people want their leader to have absolute power and divine wisdom. Germany was humiliated after World War I and a large majority of the German population elected and accepted a Dictator who promised to restore the nation's power, wealth, and prestige. The people were sitting ducks for Hitler's propaganda. Israel became jealous of other nations and dissatisfied with Gideon. Here are two illustrations of people who wanted a great King and of wiser men who opposed their desires. The Bible, as well as Eastern literature, gives clear and unmistakable warnings about the dangers of a Monarchy.

In Judges 8, the Children of Israel wanted a King like other nations had. They came to Gideon and asked him to become their King. Gideon knew what they wanted and would not become a part of a bad idea. The story tells us how Midianites had sorely oppressed the Israelites but Gideon led a small army of 300 Jews against the multitude of Midianites and defeated them, and pursued and killed them. It was a glorious military victory. The men of Israel were awed and said to Gideon: Become our King; "rule over us, both you, and your son, and your son's son also." Gideon refused their offer and sternly told them: "I will not rule over you and my son will not rule over you, THE LORD WILL RULE OVER YOU." You have judges and elders to settle your disputes and arguments but you are asking for a Sovereign with sole absolute authority like other nations have. If you have a King, he will rule with an iron hand of force and coercion. The consequences would be evil. If God rules over you, your good moral behavior, willingly practiced, without requiring the force and coercion of a Despot, is the best government. The people listened "and the country was in quietness for forty years."

The same kind of story is told in I Samuel 8 but with a different ending. The Israelites came to Samuel and asked for a King. Samuel knew it was a bad idea and had a talk with the Lord about it. The Lord told Samuel to explain to the fools what they were asking for and warn them about the consequences if they insist on having a King. Among other things, Samuel told the people: "He (the King) will take your sons, and appoint them for himself; He will appoint him captains over thousands, and captains over fifties; and will set some to plow his ground, and to reap his harvest, and to make his instruments of war, and instruments of his chariots; and he will take your daughters to be perfumers and cooks and bakers; He will take the best of your vineyards, and fields, and olive orchards and give them to his servants; He will take your menservants and maidservants, and the best of your cattle and asses and put them to his work, and he will take a tenth of your grain and flocks and you will be his slaves. And in that day you will cry out because of your King, whom you have chosen for yourselves; but the Lord will not answer you in that day." You will bitch and complain about your awful government but it will do you no good because you are getting what you asked for.

The people were stubborn and refused to listen. They were dissatisfied with Samuel because they envied what other nations had. The heathens had Kings with strong armies and were prosperous and their numbers were multiplying and they delighted in gay hedonistic fun and pleasure. The Jews had judges and elders of the tribes, but no King. They had never had a King or an Emperor and they wanted a King like the heathens had. The Jews wanted Samuel to give them their first Monarch. They insisted and told Samuel: "No! But we will have a King over us, that we may also be like all the nations, and that our King may govern us, and go out before us and fight our battles." Samuel knew they were too stubborn to listen and told the people that they could have their King.

And so the Jews had their King; and a succession of Kings and wars of conquest and became a mighty Kingdom. When their Kingdom was eventually conquered and their temple destroyed, the Jews were scattered all over the world. Since then, they have had no Kingdom and no land to call their own for two millenniums. The little patch of land that they can now call Israel is surrounded by enemies with hatred and weapons and the deadly serious intention of wiping Israel off of the map. Jewish history, like ours, could have been different.

What is the point? There is a desire within many people for someone else to take responsibility for them and that makes them want a King or Dictator or some other kind of a Despot. This is why Christ got into trouble with his own people. He would not become their military Ruler. He would not lead them into battle to establish a strong Kingdom on earth.

England still cannot entirely give up their Monarch but they eliminated their Monarchs' power to rule. Perhaps the Monarch is a tribute and symbol of the kind of Empire they once were and the staid and proper nation they want to remain.

Our founders hated the thought of being ruled by another King but our Presidents are getting close. Congressmen have been able to establish their own little realms of despotism. The seats of some senior Congressmen are plastered with epoxy. No one can pry them from their seat with a crowbar. A Congressman will give voters snake oil to remain in power. He will give a contract to a favored corporation to build jet engines for old men's rocking chairs if, in return, the corporation will make generous contributions to his campaign fund and hire his wife and son-in-law. Many sitting Senators with long term seniority have prospects for reelection that are as high as the hopes of a hound dog at a big church picnic. The congressman knows when, where, and how to use tax payers' money to benefit his constituency and himself. He knows how to make the USA one nation that is "of the government, by the government, and for the government." Some people are getting tired of all of it.

Our government shows as much trust in ordinary citizens as my cat does in that big ugly dog across the street. If a person does not have enough sense to stay away from fatty foods and to exercise now and then, he will suffer natural consequences, but I do not want my government to try to protect me, or anyone else, from the consequences of bad behavior that I have freely chosen and am responsible for. It is dumb to think that we can make a person take proper care of his body. It is dumber to think that someone else can do it for him. (Mrs. Obama, don't you have something more important to tell people than to exercise, eat right, and don't get fat?) The best government gives people the freedom to succeed or fall flat on their face, to practice good or bad habits, to eat wisely and exercise or watch television all day and night and eat like a pig. The primary purpose of government is to protect us from the lunatic in the neighborhood or in a foreign country—not to protect us from ourselves. I am not talking about morality.

I have never been arrested or jailed (except as a sailor in Tijuana) but that simply means that I am a law abiding citizen or, more likely, I am good at not getting caught. It does not mean that I am moral or immoral. Laws and the enforcement of laws are not a matter of morality. I obeyed the orders of my drill sergeant simply because I knew better than to disobey them, but my obedience was not the same as morality. Force, or the threat of force, controlled my behavior and made me tougher but did not make me a moral or immoral person. Forced, coerced, or involuntary behavior is void of moral substance. Keeping your hand out of the cookie jar just because you are afraid you will get caught has nothing to do with morality. If I obey good laws, it may reveal in me some wisdom and willingness to respect authority—but not morality.

A truly Free State requires trustworthy people. Laws and policemen are required for deviants who are dangerous to others but deviants are, hopefully, a minority of our general population. A free government is able to trust in the trustworthiness of <u>most</u> people; not all people. A good government allows free and fair competition with fair rules and honest mediators to settle disagreements. Libertarians believe that we must live under the rule of law but they want only essential laws.

Governments, like religions, try to define and designate personal behaviors as intrinsically moral or immoral; good or evil. They seem to be obsessed with making sexual behaviors illegal. When I was a boy, I was told that the devil made me do it when I was caught playing with my private parts. That instilled enough guilt to make me incurably neurotic. Bless my mother's soul; she was laughing when she said it, and that helped. My church's strict prohibitions extended to card playing, dancing, and going to movies on Sunday. I got the idea that fun was sinful. Now I am older, more carefree, and a lot more stubborn. Only my wife can tell me what to eat, drink, smoke, or how and with whom I can have sex. I, now, listen to my wife, and my kids, most of the time, just to please them; but they know that I can be deaf and incorrigible when I want to. I love the tolerance and freedom in my home. If we go to hell we will have a lot of familiar faces around; maybe even my preacher's.

I hope most of the people in our nation are trustworthy enough to survive and thrive with tons of freedom; however, like most people, I have very little trust in our present government largely because it does not have much trust in me. It is now as hard as nails to change our government because so many people are now employed by Governments and we know that their constituency is powerful in elections. This is a fundamental reason why Congressmen encounter so much resistance when they try to downsize governments. Time and again, history tells us that a government can become so big and powerful that only a revolution can change it. I wonder if the current demonstrations in the streets of our cities and the Tea Party presage some kind of a real revolution.

Lincoln became a Dictator in our first Civil War because he had to; it was the only way to fight that war. Since then, our Presidents keep edging closer to becoming Dictators. I hope that our second Civil War does not produce a dictator. Unfortunately, our former Presidents have discovered that the best way to garner dictatorial power was to convince the nation that it was in a war and, if necessary, start a little war; with or without Congressional approval. A war makes it easy for a President to shred the Constitution and Bill of Rights.

Since 1861, Presidents have routinely bypassed Congress for all sorts of wars under different names. Presidents cleverly get money for war. The Commander in Chief gives orders and the Generals have no choice but to salute and obey. I honor and respect our military and believe it must be strong. I am not opposed to war when we are in real danger and must protect ourselves. When the threat is real, we have a good and valid reason to wage war. That was not the case in the American Civil War except for the threat to the Union by secession. Most common people in the North and South did not see a threat or a reason worth the deaths of so many people. The worst carnage in our history could have been avoided. Powerful men on both sides maneuvered, pressured, and propagandized to make the war happen.

Few Americans believe that our revolution was an ignoble war. We fought to separate ourselves from England and we believe the cause was worthy of the war. Polk and Buchanan went to war for a different reason. They simply wanted expansion and more territory when we conquered Mexico. Some greedy people were sadly disappointed when we did not take all of Mexico. Some, who were less greedy, were satisfied by taking just half of Mexico. We conquered Indians to civilize and Christianize them and, along the way, began to covet the land that Indians foolishly thought belonged to them. William Penn, and some other settlers, bargained with

Indians and paid them for land, but most of the land in the lower 48 that we now proudly posses was simply taken—but not without a fight.

We had some nice little wars in the Caribbean to free places like Cuba and Haiti and to dominate the Atlantic. Then we had a bigger war in the Philippines to dominate the Pacific. What's your problem, Bob? Do you want to give it all back? Hell no! Was there any other way for our nation to grow, expand, become a great power, and establish an Empire? Hell no! I am glad we have all of our land and, unlike some, who are more moral than I am, I do not feel the least bit guilty about expanding our Empire. We simply behaved in the way that most normal ambitious human beings and nations do in similar situations. I just hope we remember the dangers of greedy expansion, ego driven ambition and misused aggression. I also think it would be better if we were a little more honest about our wars. Lying about Korea, Viet Nam, and our most recent wars has gotten us into a hell of a mess. Civilizations and Governments die just as men do. Some die by natural causes and some by man-made causes. Most die by a combination of the two.

I have clearly revealed my bias for a Libertarian type Government in domestic affairs but, not necessarily, foreign affairs. I know a Libertarian government may not be possible in the foreseeable future. However, I would like to see us moving in the direction of more, rather than fewer, freedoms. We have reached a level of expansive and restrictive government that many, I hope most, people believes is too burdensome and many of us want reforms; and an influential portion of our population wants *drastic* reforms. Are we about to see the pendulum swing in a different direction? How did we get where we are?

CHAPTER FOURTEEN

THE ROAD TO IMPERIALISM

Do your children know the story of our founding fathers? Do they know how hard the fight was against England and how close we came to losing? Do your children know how they wanted to be free from a stubborn King and fashion a government that would protect their new nation from another Despot? Many children know about as much about our political history as I do about advanced calculus.

After we won our freedom, the first big question was "what kind of government shall we have?" Our Constitution was a squeaker and came close to not being enacted and ratified. Its composition and passage in the convention required months of arguments, debates, long passionate speeches, heated battles about the Central Government and States' rights. Even the prior Articles of Confederation was hard to achieve because States were apprehensive and jealous of their independence and reluctant to join the Confederation.

The passage of our Constitution and Bill of Rights required many give and take compromises and reassurances to the thirteen States that they would not be swallowed whole and lose their sovereignty. It passed, was ratified and produced a limited viable Central Government. Those documents put in writing the power, authority, restrictions and limitations of our Federal Government and the separate States. Madison and Hamilton were dissatisfied with the Constitution but believed it was the best they could get. They wanted a much stronger Central Government and wanted the States to have minimal authority, power, and jurisdiction. Hamilton and Madison would be pleased today because few people now pay much attention to the Constitution and Bill of Right.

The Constitution is routinely treated like rubbish by Presidents, Supreme Courts, and, to a much lesser degree, by our poor enfeebled Congressmen. The President bypasses Congress and thumbs his nose at the

Constitution by his powers of Executive Orders and Executive Privilege. The President now has allies in the Federal Bureaus and Agencies that enforce his disregard for Congress. The Supreme Court now exercises supreme powers not granted to them in the Constitution. They violate the Constitution with each Judicial Review of a Congressional Acts. The Supreme Court now almost routinely reviews acts of Congress and decisions by lower Courts. It strikes down laws passed by the representatives of the people in Congress, thereby making the vote and will of the people null and void. Congress has been reduced to a wimp and has been unwilling to fight to regain Constitutional Congressional powers, authority, and responsibilities. Will they ever fight to reclaim and restore a representative Government? Have we forgotten? Remember; our Constitution and Bill of Rights were supposed <u>to protect us from the government rather than to protect the government from us.</u> Being a Democracy doesn't automatically make us, or any other nation, free and tolerant. We once had good reasons to be proud of the freedoms in the USA; but I am frightened by the speed of their disappearance. Where can we find another Thomas Jefferson?

Gore Vidal traces the rise of the Supreme Court toward Imperial power. The rise began with *Marbury v Madison* in 1803. A quarrel developed between President Jefferson and Mr. Marbury, who was appointed to an office by Jefferson's predecessor just before leaving office. President Jefferson ordered Secretary Madison to remove Marbury and replace him. Mr. Marbury took it to court. He insisted that Section 13 of Congress's Judiciary Act of 1789 protected him. Chief Justice Marshall decided in favor of the President by declaring that Section 13 of Congress's Judiciary Act of 1789 was unconstitutional. This set a precedent for the Supreme Court. From then on, the Supreme Court could cite precedence to declare Acts of Congress unconstitutional and make them null and void.

Hamilton loved the Court's action. He argued loudly and speciously in favor of the Court. Congress complained that its powers had been usurped but bowed—as it has been bowing ever since then except for two feeble attempts to reassert its Constitutional duty and authority. Now the Court could regulate Congress instead of Congress regulating the Court as stipulated in the Constitution. The Constitution clearly gives Congress the power to regulate the Court—and not the other way around. We have been traveling the other way around for a long time. Remember:

Article III of the Constitution clearly states: "The Supreme Court shall have appellate jurisdiction, both as to law and fact, with such exceptions and <u>under such regulations as the Congress</u> shall make.

Let me repeat: The Constitution clearly states that Congress shall regulate the appellate jurisdiction of the Supreme Court and place exceptions on its appellate powers. It does not say that the Supreme Court can regulate Congress and declare its legislation null and void. Now, the votes and will of the people carry less power.

The Supreme Judges' rise gathered more momentum when Judge Marshall, speaking for the majority, in *Barron v. City of Baltimore,* boldly declared that the Bill of Rights was binding only upon the federal government and not upon the states. What's that? State and local governments don't have to be bothered by the Bill of Rights? Thanks to the Supreme Court; the Bill of Rights was ignored for many decades. It was another stride in denuding the rights and power of the people. Now the rise of an Imperial Supreme Court had the wind at its back.

On March 6, 1857, Chief Justice Roger Brooke Taney, read the infamous Dred Scott decision and put the power and domain of the Supreme Court in a higher gear. The Court reviewed another act of Congress, the Missouri Compromise, and declared it, unconstitutional. Poor Judge Taney has been maligned and badly misunderstood. He did that because he was racist and wanted to defend slavery; right? Wrong!

Taney was an 81 year old former Attorney General and Secretary of the Treasury under President Jackson. He had an unblemished reputation. In earlier years he had inherited slaves on his Maryland plantation but set all of them free except for three who were too old to work. He kept these on his plantation to support them in their old age. He was not motivated by an animus toward the black race. The issue was about a runaway slave but the history making legal consequences of the trial had much less to do with slavery than it did with the escalating powers of the Supreme Court and the rapidly declining powers and freedom of the people. Once again, an act of Congress was declared unconstitutional and made null and void. This decision had a direct influence on the conflicts that erupted into our civil war.

Dear old Judge Taney may not have realized that he was swinging the flood gates open even wider, for the Supreme Court to make acts of congress null and void. Few people now know, or even care about the fact, that the Supreme Court spits on the Constitution every time it reviews an Act of Congress. It happens so frequently, we may wonder why Congress even considers introducing an act without, first, taking it to the Supreme Court to review. The President can check Congress with the power of his veto and the people can vote a Congressman out of office but there are no checks on the Supreme Court without changing the Constitution. The Supreme Court now has effectively shredded the Constitution and made Congress a eunuch. There are now essentially no restraints on the Supreme Court's natural tendency to expand its powers and steal the prerogatives of Congress. Now the Supreme Court can handily mold and shape the nation in its own image oblivious to the wishes of the people.

Hamilton would applaud the actions of our Courts and Presidents that disregard our Constitution. Thomas Jefferson is turning over in his grave. From March, 1865 to 1970, ninety acts of Congress were held void in whole or part.

The rise of Presidential Imperialism is the second act in the odyssey of centralized power. The Constitution devised a series of checks and balances that placed limitations and prohibitions on any President who yearned for dictatorial powers. Lincoln has the "distinction" of becoming the first President to blatantly set aside the Constitution. He justified his action as necessary to wage war. Congressman Lincoln said, in 1847, that any state has the moral and constitutional right to govern itself but he changed his mind when he became President.

Vidal describes the transformation like this: "The first republic was a loose confederation of thirteen autonomous states (and remained pretty much that way) until 1862, when the American Bismarck, Abraham Lincoln, took the mystical position that no state could ever leave the Union. When the southern states disagreed a bloody war was fought. On his own authority, he levied troops and made war; took unappropriated money from the treasury; suspended habeas corpus. When the aged Chief Justice Taney hurled the constitution at his head, the president ducked." How did Lincoln break out of the constitutional cage? He used the presidential oath as a hammer to knock down the bars. Thus he placed in the hands of his successors the powerful tools of inherent executive privilege and executive orders—making the restraints of the Constitution and Bill Of Rights thinner than tissue paper. Grant's wife called it a silly old nuisance.

The Office of the President began its rise to Imperial stature in a much more sudden and dramatic fashion than the Supreme Court. Our nation became an instantaneous over-night full grown dictatorship in 1861. Lincoln imprisoned thousands of dissenters without a hearing, took money from the National Treasury without authorization, and waged war before getting Congressional permission. Deserters were executed without a trial. Central authority in Washington D. C. became a runaway train that has slowed down a few times in the following century and a half but has never been halted. The exalted escalation of Presidential power began with an explosion. Its escalation continues with Executive Privilege, Executive Power, and Executive Orders that ignore our poor impotent Congress. Since Lincoln, Presidents have issued executive orders more than 12,000 times. They are now commonplace because the current President issues them like passing out candy to children on Halloween. I wonder how long it will take us to erect a throne in the Oval Office. Lincoln surely did not know what he was starting. Maybe he would have let the seceded State go in peace if he had known.

Lincoln wanted to preserve the Union and he did with a shotgun marriage. When the war was over he told the nation that he wanted friendly reunion with all of the seceded States. I could be wrong, but I believe that he wanted the States and local governments to retain the authority and freedom that the Constitution gives them—and he did not want the Federal Government to harass and oppress them. Radical politicians passed Congressional Acts of Enforcement that were designed to empower and legitimize Union troops and officials to use force to prop up the Federal officials in the South and to wage war against organized white resistance; but, thank heavens, the Supreme Court nullified some of them. The only era when Congress ran roughshod over Presidents was in the immediate aftermath of the war. President Johnson fought radical Congressmen and lost. That Congressional power evaporated a decade later. Presidential power did not evaporate. With the opportunities of a war or two (or five or six), here and there, our Presidents found a fool-proof way to keep their exalted powers. All a President needs is a nice little war to ignore Congress and the Constitution. Now you tell me; have our Presidents made us a war-like nation?

CHAPTER FIFTEEN

FREEDOM AND PREJUDICE

"They own me", the black maid said; and she was right. The movie, *The Help*, will certainly be nominated for the best motion picture of 2011. One of the maids in the motion picture tells a black friend that her employer died and the employer designated in her will that the maid would work for an obnoxious daughter after her death. The maid had hoped she would become the maid of a nice daughter of her deceased employer, but the will designated that she would work for a different daughter; a hateful daughter. The maid said she had no choice. If she did not work for the hateful daughter, the family would put out the word and she would not be able to find employment with anyone else. That is when the maid said, "They own me." Her only choice was to work for the hateful daughter or be unemployed.

The movie was set in the 1950s and contained a mixture of facts and myths. Most of the public will probably accept the myths in the movie as facts. In one scene, the movie portrayed twenty or so Southern white women at a bridge party in Jackson, Mississippi, and any normal person who sees the movie will detest the women. They are shallow, arrogant, egotistical, conceited, skinny, prim and proper, over dressed with exquisite coiffures, and exceedingly racist. They make insulting remarks about black people in private conversations and in the presence of maids. All normal people will despise the women. They are portrayed as typical of middle and upper class Mississippi women in the 1950s; and most of the public will probably buy it as accurate and factual. The heroine is an exception that genuinely cares about the plight of the maids and writes *The Help* to expose racism and mistreatment of black people in Mississippi. The maids in the movie care for the women's children from birth through adolescences and become attached to the children with love; and the children love them. The good relationships continue into adulthood. This

141

part of the movie is factual. The part about the typical Mississippi woman feeling awkward with her babies and neglecting them is prejudicial myth.

The predominant attitude of the maids toward the white women is resentful. They abhor the women and, in private conversations with other maids, mock them as the empty-headed, inept phonies that they are in the movie. There is an exception of one maid employed by a "white trash" woman who lives alone and is wealthy, but is an alcoholic emotional basket case. The maid is welcomed by the ostracized woman who has no racism and treats the maid well. The maid becomes a teacher, counselor, and companion to her employer and helps the woman grow up and overcome her problems. Practically all of the other white women treat their maids with disrespect and the maids return the favor. The maids are trapped in an underclass and see themselves enslaved by their race and circumstances. That part is factual. Racism in Mississippi, and every other State, is fact. The prevalent personal individual relationships between maids and the families they worked for are portrayed in the movie in ways that are much, much, more myth than fact. My long time good Yankee friends insist that it is facts. I had four sisters and only one of them could afford a maid in the 50s and 60s and anyone who says my sister and her maid did not genuinely love and respect each other are ignorant.

Any modern conversation about freedom, slavery, prejudice, and racism in the 1800s and today can be meaningful and helpful only if we take the advice of Socrates and carefully define our words and their meanings. In ways that are seldom recognized, the racist white women in *The Help* were more enslaved and less free than the black women. The maids were enslaved in a perpetual underclass that the white women in the movie were not concerned about.

So, what is your understanding of freedom? I am free to the extent that I am not forced, coerced, intimidated, or seduced into saying or doing something against my will—as long as my actions do not harm another person or seriously threaten the State. This also applies to social groups, including churches, temples, and synagogues. I am free when I can make my own decisions and choose my behaviors without needless and unwanted restrictions. Sometimes I restrict my own open expressions of certain ideas and emotions out of consideration for other people when I have good will and behave wisely. I regret the numerous times when I acted with ill will and ignorance. I do not believe that everyone dislikes unnecessary restrictions imposed on their freedom by someone or something outside of them.

It is normal and natural to dislike a highly restrictive and overbearing government. Of course, everyone has to give up some individual freedoms to belong to a society. Wise, reasonable, and necessary restriction are necessary for the good of the society we live in. Sometimes restrictions have to be accepted as the lesser of two evils. I will pay my income tax rather than go to jail, but both options are undesirable. Of course, no one can be totally and completely free in every way? That is not the problem.

Some of my restrictions are imposed on me by my obsessive compulsive personality. Psychotherapy has helped but I will never be completely cured. I will always be a workaholic; often to my wife's chagrin. Many restrictions are self-imposed in different ways. Inside a person, a master of slaves can become the slave of his slaves; a factory owner can become a slave of his factory workers; a prisoner can be freer than his jailer. This means that freedom and bondage are not simple words with one simple meaning and both must be qualified to clarify their meanings. A plantation slave's smile may be a forced smile; a pretense to avoid mistreatment. The smile can also be genuine, free, and a spontaneous expression of a good relationship with his master.

What is your understanding of slavery and bondage? Perhaps it is enough to say that slavery or bondage is the opposite of all that is said above about freedom but that would omit a fact about human autonomy. I interviewed a prisoner to make a mental assessment of him for his public defender. The prisoner was confined in one small cell, alone, in the maximum security section of the prison in Florence, Colorado. No prisoner could see another prisoner while he was in his cell, but each prisoner was allowed to leave his cell and walk around in a common area of the unit for one hour a day. During that time they could see and converse with other prisoners. The prisoner that I interviewed had managed to get out of his cell while another prisoner was in the common area and stab him to death with a makeshift knife. I could not truthfully say that the prisoner had no autonomy or choice about his actions unless he was severely psychotic.

Severe psychosis can rob a person of all autonomy or capacity for choice. The prisoner I interviewed was not psychotic. This prisoner in a small cell, retained some autonomy; some choice of his behaviors and responses to other people before he broke out of his cell. Beyond psychosis, it is difficult to think of anyone in any situation that does not have some measure of autonomy and choice; no matter how severely restricted he may be by external confinement. My point is that bondage and slavery are immensely different in degree and form. A mother on welfare may be restricted from marriage by the threat of losing welfare assistance. Poor families may be restricted from moving out of a slum by economics. Bondage can mean that a person is so deep in debt he can never get out. St. Peter don't you call me cause I can't go; I owe my soul to the company store. Bondage and slavery can be voluntary or involuntary; intentional or unintentional.

Two people in a sadomasochistic relationship can actually experience weird pleasure by being tied to a post, dominated, whipped, and punished emotionally and physically. They may be trapped by their neurosis and unable to get out of the bond without help. Christians call themselves voluntary servants of Christ and Muslims are voluntary martyrs for Allah. Perry Como sang about being a prisoner of love. Obsessive romantics extol the compulsive pain and pleasure of "being in love."

Many think of marriage as a voluntary owning and belonging; even though radical feminists have a much different view of marriage. They have called it legalized slavery or forced servitude. The owner of the Dallas Cowboys buys and owns his players but I doubt if the players call themselves involuntary slaves; even though they are bought, sold, and owned. (There was, however, one professional player who recently referred to himself as a slave during the bargaining between owners and the players union.) Labor Unions were organized to help coal miners who were powerless to change their circumstances without an organization and were like hostages without choice before the union was organized. Bondage wears many disguises and is a reality that severely restricts the freedom of many people.

The Wikipedia Encyclopedia says: "The number of slaves today remains as high as 12 million to 27 million, though this is probably the smallest proportion of the world's population in history. (If we accept a broader definition of bondage and slavery, the number is ten times higher.) Most are debt slaves, largely in South Asia, who are under debt bondage incurred by lenders, sometimes, even for generations. The worst kind of modern human trafficking sells women and children for prostitutes into sex industries. Slavery is a system in which people are the property of others. Slaves can be held against their will from the time of their capture, purchase, or birth, and deprived of the right to leave, to refuse to work, or to demand compensation."

During the Congressional Reconstruction, radical Congressmen tried to replace black slavery with another form of bondage. Union troops restricted and controlled Southern white people. Officials of the Federal government, with the enforcement power of Union troops, placed black men and Republicans in government offices in formerly seceded States to give the black race and Republicans political power. The Federal government enacted legislation to give public land owned by the Federal government and land owned by white Southerners to black families. Federal officials tried to rearrange and change Southern society and racial relationships and the eventual consequences were disastrous for both races.

It is a biological impossibility for even identical twins to be completely physically, emotionally, mentally, and socially equal. A good society will strive for more equality and less inequality between races and classes of people but if it is forced it becomes artificial and phony. As soon as Union troops went home, the society was segregated as much as, or more than, before the war and white domination was infused with a new animosity. Here lies a sad ugly con on the black race. Lincoln, the war, and reconstruction did <u>not</u> free the black race in the South or North; except in their legal status.

Martin Luther King and Civil Rights legislation eliminated forced segregation in the 1950s and 60s and gave the black race freedom from a legal restriction; but most of us know that the black race is still not as free as the white race and much of the reason can be traced back to misused force in the 1800s. The nation's right answer to the problem of black bondage was not then, and is not now, to employ force to <u>make</u> all black men and women free and equal to all white people. Forced segregation can be wisely prevented but integration and assimilation that is real and helpful to either, or both, races, must be desired by both races, freely chosen, and come from the heart. Only then can it lift all races. I believe Christ was right about the crucial issue of the heart.

In his lifetime, Mohammed, the first prophet of Islam, was wiser than were the radical Congressmen in the 1800s. Mohammed lived a modest simple life after he became the supreme ruler and Islam was usually tolerant of other religions after their Empire was firmly established in the 8th century. Mohammed knew that it was in Islam's best interests to be friendly with religions that posed no threat to him. In the 9th century, the

Islam Empire was far more tolerant of protestant Christians and Jews in Spain, and other places, than was the Roman Catholic Church. That may be hard for many of us to believe today while so many Muslims kill each other and want to kill us.

All normal people want to move up and want the freedom to be able to move as high as their talent, intellect, and ability allow them to rise. This is a normal and natural impulse. Adler erected a psychology on this human trait. When the natural human impulse to rise is allowed to motivate behaviors in a free and open society, humans develop a normal stratification of positions in their society. When Kings, governments, and religions tried to artificially manipulate social positions, the societies that they manufactured eventually malfunctioned. They assumed hubris above God and the laws of creation. The valid role of government is not to establish an elite class and protect their position in society; even though that happens much too often. The valid role of government is to reward merit and protect the lame and low elements of a society from abuse by those above them; and try to give as many people as possible fair opportunities to succeed or fail by their own merit. Blood lines should matter only if the blood line endows a person with genuine superior qualities.

When a person or race cannot rise higher, the reason may be natural or artificial. I tried to reach a starting position on my college football team; I made the team but never became a starter; my usual and natural position was a bench warmer. My failure to rise no higher than a bench warmer was not due to an artificial barrier; both the coach and I knew that I was a natural bench warmer. If the coach made me an artificial starter, he would hurt the team and me too. I would have been resentful if I thought I had more ability than I actually had and the coach was unfairly holding me back. Unfortunately, many people are resentful about their place in our society because they wrongly believe someone is holding them back. Even more unfortunately, many people are artificially held back by other people and governments. Plato based his philosophy on the premise that people have a natural and right position in society and in a good society people will be able to find, fill, and accept their place.

In a human society, people give different meanings to the idea of "higher". St. Francis is a good example of a person whose perception of higher was different from most people. St. Francis perceived higher as a life of piety and self-imposed poverty. Feminists in the 60s correctly believed their gender was artificially held back by patriarchy, and fought to gain a higher position in society. The first necessary step was to make women dissatisfied with their social position and angry enough about artificial barriers to fight them. They fought well and barriers were eliminated. Their perception of "higher" molded the thinking and behaviors of a generation of women; for better and for worse. When a large segment of a society is dissatisfied and angry about their position, we have the dynamics of a revolution. Every chicken knows his or her place in the pecking order and males fight about it once in awhile but hens wisely accept theirs. They have a social instinct that lets them know their position and be content with it. Does this mean that chickens are wiser than people?

Some unwanted forms of bondage are self-imposed; sometime intentionally and sometime unintentionally. One of the most common examples is a bad marriage. A wife or husband can become unhappily dominated and want out; but feel trapped. A young girl with an unintentional pregnancy can find herself trapped in difficult circumstances. Young people find themselves in a prison where they do not want to be as an unintended consequence of foolish behavior. A gullible cult followed a lunatic to Jonestown with no intention of dying by poisoning. Unintended bondage is often the consequence of bad choices.

I believe, however, that the worst traps and barriers to upward mobility are artificial and manmade. They are the fruits of pernicious prejudice, racism, and selfish perceptions of people as objects to be used; and, sometime, abused by sadists. Pernicious prejudice is spawned by ignorance, irrational emotions, learned ill will, and false preconceived ideas about people. They instill an "us against them" mentality. This mentality is more than just a poor attitude and is much too common in races and classes of people in our nation; and is bad enough now to frighten many people. The mind set is obvious in politics and religions and the fighting has become so low and ugly, it makes rational friendly cooperation impossible among people where it is the most needed. How can people in our nation become friendly and cooperative neighbors; working together for themselves and others, when large classes of people are angry at each other and antagonistic?

Who are the worst culprits? I am convinced that out government is the premiere erector of artificial man made obstacles to freedom and opportunities of the under classes for upward social and economic mobility in our nations. Our government excels in erecting legal barriers and social programs that stand in the way of people who could, and would, move up, in a freer society. There are some who would move up in a free society and some who, by choice and personal characteristics, would not. I am afraid that resistance to meaningful integration is stronger in the black, than the white, race. I am convinced that the reason is culture more than color.

Last night I watched and listened to the New York Philharmonic Orchestra performing in the Lincoln Center. The conductor and every instrument player were White or Asian. I earnestly and sincerely wished that I could see a black man conducting the orchestra and black men and women playing instruments in the orchestra. I wished there were as many black performers as a percentage that was equal to their percentage of the nation's population. At the moment, I wished that I was wealthy and could become a patron of a black boy and a black girl who were musically talented and had a wish to play in the New York Philharmonic, or some other orchestra like it. The instrument players are not highly paid but love the music. The only thing I would rather give a lot of money to is the church that I attended as a boy.

All of the men and women in our Philosophical Café would love to have black people become regular members of the Café but, if a black person attends the Café a few times, he soon drops out and the Café remains all white. I believe the reason is mostly because he is the only black person among thirty white people. The reason may also be cultural. I wish that someday white churches would reach out to black churches to periodically exchange preachers, choirs, and portions of their congregations for worship services and other activities; and vice versa. I am afraid that Reverend Wright would strongly resist the idea.

We have witnessed the fact that it is possible for ill-will to be transformed into good-will. Look at the nation's relationships with Germany and Japan today. How did this happen? Our conflicting interests were transformed into mutual interests after the war. Does this kind of transformation require a war? I hope not. Our children and grandchildren will have a future molded largely by our future relationships with China and other great nations. Relationships must become more neighborly and cooperative than antagonistic for a bright future. I do not believe that a Professor in a classroom can transform national and racial relationships. I believe that it can be accomplished only by mutually beneficial trade and by direct personal interaction and communication.

Good things usually happen when individuals and groups get together in voluntary and enjoyable ways. It is hard to be prejudiced against someone that you know personally; you may not like the person but ignorant prejudice does not make you dislike him. More often than not, if the setting and atmosphere is good, personal interaction will engender beneficial knowledge and positive emotions among people who freely get together. If it is possible to plan and promote direct personal interaction and communication, it may be an effective way to eliminate racism and prejudice.

Racism and prejudice are reduced and friendly relationships develop naturally in military service. The races have a common mission and need each other but, just as importantly, they live together and know each other personally. We do not prejudge a person that we know personally. We may, or may not, want to be that person's friend but it will not be because we have prejudged that person. I had good black friends in Louisiana but it was not enough to eliminate my prejudice against a race.

Humans have a natural tendency to view a stranger with suspicion. In the earliest beginnings of our species, our social groups were small and probably remained separate from other groups. When we became humans, our groups became larger and began interaction with other groups more frequently. How wide does survival want our social group to become; and with how much interaction? This is where religions have been influential. Some religions jealously guard their group's identity with rituals, traditions, common beliefs, and warnings about involvement with other groups. That can be valuable to the groups' survival but also divisive in a multicultural nation. Some religions diminish the importance of separate group identity and promote nationwide, or universal, inclusion of all humans in one large society.

Most of us experience personal value by inclusion in, and loyalty to, a unique identifiable group that we can say is "my group". Can we keep the value of belonging to this separate group and also belong, and be loyal to, one world and a universal society. This is now a human dilemma in which diversity clashes with nationality, especially when diversity clashes with the essential value and necessity of a recognized and accepted core culture and language. Nationality clashes with some people's desire for all nations to meld into one world. A one world vision is frightening to many people and I do not know how much the fear is, or is not, valid and justified. However, we are many generations away from the possibility of one universal society; if it ever becomes a reality.

There will probably always be a form of individual and group prejudice in social creatures, including humans, that is benign and essential to survival. It is a natural preference to be in the company of people we are accustomed to; people who resemble us. If three herds of cattle are grazing on a wide expanse of land and a thunderstorm causes them to stampede and the herds become intermingled; soon after the storm, all of the cattle will spontaneously seek out members of their own herd, and soon three mixed herds will again become three separate herds. It is a phenomenon of social group value that naturally evolved. All social species depend on it for survival. This is a social instinct that is often used by human societies to manufacture pernicious prejudice.

The people that study animals know that existential circumstances naturally cause increased or decreased conflicts within social groups. The simple and well known social dynamics apply to humans as well as other animals. Conflicts decrease when there is plenty of available food for all; they increase when food is scarce. This has a direct bearing on the wisdom and foolishness of our social welfare programs. The programs are horrific in many ways but essential; until the nation has better alternatives to make certain people do not go hungry. I believe better alternatives are possible. The programs create a prejudice in many people in our nation toward people on welfare. We see current demonstrations of violence and hostile competition in nations, like Africa, where people are starving and their hunger becomes a breeding ground for genocide and Despots.

I believe we could have a better world if we could identify and separate pernicious prejudice from benign prejudice. The players on the Denver Broncos football team form positive relationships and a good strong team bond; especially if they are winning. The players don't give a damn about skin color if their team mate is a good player who helps them win. Negative prejudice can be buried beneath team spirit, team morale, and their need of each other to play the best game possible. Negative prejudice toward the Oakland Raiders is a different matter. As a Bronco fan, I hate those damned Oakland Raiders. In this case, my prejudice and hate are normal, natural, and enjoyable—and has no affect on the Raiders.

Winning is a key to the team bond. A team that is losing every game more easily becomes dissatisfied with individual members of the team; and so can the fans. When the Broncos were losing, the fans booed quarterback Kyle Orton. This is an analogy for nations that are succeeding or failing. People who perceive our nation "losing" are likely to blame the President.

Democrats blame Republicans and vice versa. The desire to blame goes away if we think our nation is "winning".

I was too young to know anything about politics during our great depression but I do remember that it was not divisive among common ordinary people because we were one in the same boat. There was a spirit among common people during the depression to help each other get through it. Our house became more crowded with kin folks. A black couple asked if they could live in our barn, the only space not already occupied, and my parents readily said that they could and they were not asked to pay for rent. I do not see that spirit today even though numerous families have to live together. I was too young to know if the politicians played a rampant blame game during the depression but I know the blame game is being played viciously today. During World War II, the whole nation faced a grave threat from a clearly known common enemy and it bonded us together as one nation working together like a team. Today, our wars are tearing us apart.

These simple lessons from nature broaden the definition of prejudice. They tell us how, why, and when prejudice is benign and beneficial or malignant and destructive. However, any form of prejudice is pre-judging a person, or class of people, before we really know them. It becomes easier to falsely demonize or foolishly idolize someone. With vicious propaganda, we dehumanize people perceived as an enemy. Let me repeat, the best remedy for prejudice is to learn as much as we can about people that is true and valid before we judge them. Our false ideas about people can be mild or gross; benign or malignant.

When we come face-to-face with an actual problem, men usually try to think of something they can do to fix the problem. When we have problems in personal relationships, they cannot be "fixed". If a good relationship is possible, the only requirement is to get negative things out of the way that prevent a good relationship from natural fruition; and let it happen. We may need to talk openly with the other person about problems to eliminate them. If my offer of a relationship with another person is responded to with suspicion and hostility, I just forget about the person if the relationship is not important, but, if the relationship is important that is when I must talk, act, or do something to get the negatives our of the way.

The same principles apply to prejudice and racism between black and white people? We can enjoy good racial relationships if we remove prejudice, suspicion and ignorance. When black and white people get together, talk, and get to know each other, good relationships will naturally develop. I hope Abraham Lincoln and Louis Farrakhan are wrong about colonization. The Nation of Islam believes that the black and white races need to be separated and the USA should provide a country, or part of a country, where black people can have a separate nation. I hope most black people in the USA believe they can hold their own, in a multi-racial, multi-cultural, multi-religious, and tolerant nation if prejudice and road blocks can be removed and fair opportunities to rise are plentiful and open to everyone.

CHAPTER SIXTEEN

WOMENS' POWER

Pray tell me if you will,
Why man and woman get along so ill?
Mephistopheles

The sly old Devil was up to his usual tricks. He knew the answer before he asked the question and was taunting poor old Faust. Conflicts of interests between males and females are natural and will always cause problems. Professor Edwin O. Wilson was almost tarred and feathered by his colleagues in 1970 for stating a fact; a fact that should by now be obvious; gender differences are more than just biological and gender conflicts began with the first sexually reproducing organisms. Wilson added another obvious reality; sex introduced an antisocial compulsion in society and is the instigator of much fighting. Can we blame gender conflicts for starting the Civil War? Of course, we cannot. I know that women are the root of all evil, even though my wife and female friends stoutly disagree and call me bad names.

Seriously speaking, no one should ever underestimate how much the intellect, influence, and powers of women have directed the course of human history. Men do it at their peril and women should know it and be proud. I have often said you can judge the level of civilization in a culture or nation by the level of social status and power that women have. Many times the power of just one woman has changed history. Let me give you one example.

I think of this story as a morality play in which a young woman's morals are seen through different prisms. Her enemies called her Madame Whore because they envied and hated her and she actually was adulterous. She had beauty, a superb mind, immense will power, superior talents, ambition, sex appeal, and she wanted to become the next "declared mistress" of King

Louis XV. She needed all of these attributes and more to compete with the most beautiful women in France for the coveted privileges and status of the position. Louis had mistresses before and after Jeanne but all of them pale into insignificance when compared to the power she gained and the influence she wielded in 18th century France. Madame de Chateauroux, his former mistress, had died unexpectedly while still young leaving Louis with a broken heart. Everyone knew he would soon select another woman to replace her.

Her name was Jeanne Antoinette Poisson and, when the King gave her a large estate, she became the Marquise de Pompadour. She is best known in history as Madame Pompadour but I will refer to her simply as Jeanne. Historian Will Durant said: "She was one of the most remarkable women in history, dowered with such beauty and grace as blinded most men to her sins, and yet with such powers of mind that for a brilliant decade she governed France, protected Voltaire, saved Diderot's Encyclopedie, and led the philosophies to claim her as one of their own." Without her Voltaire could not have been Voltaire and the history of 18th century France would have been sadly different.

Jeanne was born in 1721 into a bourgeois family with limited income. From the time she was a small child until her death, Jeanne heard glowing praise of her beauty, talent, and personality. She was special and she knew it and so did her mother and everyone else who met her. Her mother knew her daughter would need the best available education and training to realize her extraordinary potential and that would be expensive. Her father, M. Poisson, was languishing in Hamburg, hiding from the hangman, but her mother, Mme. Poisson, was the much loved mistress of a rich farmer general, M. de Tournehem. He loved Jeanne and insisted that she had the best tutors and teachers in Europe and gladly supplied all the money needed. Many believe he was probably the biological father of Jeanne. Jeanne loved him and always thought of him as a father. She called him oncle Tournehem. M. Poisson was persuaded to accept reality like a gentleman and refrain from making a scene about his wife's lover.

Jeanne soon rivaled the brightest stars in France in singing, dancing, acting, elocution, and intellect. When Jeanne was nine years old, a fortune teller, with remarkable prescience, marveled at Jeanne's beauty and talents and predicted that she would someday be a King's mistress. (She could not be the King's wife because marriages were political arrangements to weld national alliances and Jeanne was bourgeois.) Her mother boasted that

Jeanne was "a morsel for a King" and, when the time was right, did her part to make it happen. When Jeanne was eighteen she needed a husband and M. de Tournehem persuaded Jeanne to marry his nephew, M. d'Etioles, who fathered her two children. Jeanne was happy in her marriage and vowed that "no one in the world but the King, himself, would make her unfaithful to her husband." When Madame de Chateauroux died, Jeanne's mother already had plans for the exception to become a reality.

Mme. Poisson knew the King often hunted in the forest of Senart and she arranged for Jeanne to ride by in a lovely phaeton where the King would see her. In February, 1745, the King gave a masked ball to celebrate the marriage of the Dauphin and, at the ball, saw Jeanne's beautiful face up close for the first time. When she spoke to the King, he asked her to remove her mask and she did for a moment and then danced away. A month later he saw her again at a play given by an Italian troupe at Versailles and, a few days later, invited her to a supper. Jeanne accepted the invitation and knew it would be her opportunity to capture the King. She knew about his sexual appetite and intentions and gladly surrendered. Louis offered her an apartment at Versailles and she moved into modest accommodations that he visited every night. Jeanne also knew she must offer more than sex to gain and consolidate the place she wanted in the King's life, his court, and the power she coveted.

Louis was moody, indecisive, and shirked the burdens of a King. He did not like the demands of government or the court for his attention. Besides sex, his passions were hunting and gambling. Jeanne knew he was easily bored and depressed and she created new entertainments and diversions in Versailles that pleased Louis. She established a little theater and staged plays in which the best actors, actresses, and musicians in France performed and Jeanne always took the leading role. Her singing and acting were superb. Louis felt at ease with her and could be himself with her more than in any other setting. She became his sole confident and he began placing in her hands the demands of government. Soon access to all court commissions, official patronage, and appointments to coveted positions came through her.

No one believed Jeanne could ever become the King's *maitresse declare* because she came from a bourgeois family but the king arranged for her to have an estate of her own and the title of Madame de Pompadour and, when she was presented to the court, the Queen accepted her as a necessary reality and invited her to dinner. Her enemies made insulting comments and circulated insults: "A little bourgeois, raised to be a slut, brings everything down to her level, and makes the court a slum." She wrote Voltaire: "I treat all these horrors with the most complete disdain and I am, in fact, very serene knowing that it is my work for peace, my contribution to the happiness of humanity that inspires their wrath."

The King was now her loving captive and never left her side as a faithful ally. He depended on Jeanne as he depended on no one else to relieve his boredom and to shoulder for him the responsibilities of government. When their sexual relationship waned and she could no longer "rise to the King's heat", Louis still needed and wanted her and other arrangements were made to satisfy his sexual appetite. They rented a little house on the edge of Versailles called the Park-aux-Cerf where a harem of young girls, recruited by his valet, resided. These girls had to be young and virgins to "make sure they were free from a venereal disease." Rumor has it that they were sometimes as young as nine or ten.

For their rendezvous with Louis, the girls were taken to the rooms of Lebel, the King's valet du chambre. The room was nicknamed "the Birdcage" because "one takes young girls there." If a girl became pregnant and bore a child (he had at least seven illegitimate children) the King made sure that the financial needs of the girl and child was well provided for. Whether or not, Jeanne was complicate, she kept her silence. She knew they posed no threat to her place beside the King or in the government. She said that these little uneducated girls could share his bed because she knew she had his heart. (Jeanne became pregnant several times by Louis but always miscarried.)

Jeanne hired the best architect to design and build beautiful chalets for the King's retreats and hunting lodge. She amassed wealth and property for herself and family. Louis gave her spacious apartments which she adorned with the finest furniture, drapes, and art. She had Boucher and Vanloo paint the ceiling of her boudoir with voluptuous goddesses of love. She established a larger theater at Versailles and spent extravagant sums of money supporting artists, musicians, painters, and architecture. She even rescued minor arts and made them a vital asset to French culture. She gave commissions to more than a hundred artists. When the King tried to hold her back, she took his place as patron. She created her own renaissance of art in France and, under King Louis XV and Jeanne, France reached its highest point of influence on the culture of European civilization.

Jeanne was spiting up blood from tuberculosis at the age of fifteen and her health gradually weakened. She made Francois Quesnay her personal physician and gave him a suite of rooms directly under her own. This is where she, also, entertained and conversed with philosophers. Among the philosophers were Diderot, d'Alembert, Duclos, Helvetius, and Turgot whose thinking was considered dangerous and heretical by the Pope and would also have frightened the King. When Voltaire was repeatedly rebuffed by the Pope in his attempts to gain admission to the French Academy, Jeanne pleaded with the Pope until he finally relented and agreed to Voltaire's admission. Voltaire and Jeanne corresponded and remained friends until her death. Jeanne was easily the most cultured woman of her time. She read as often as she could and accumulated a library of more than 3000 volumes.

While Jeanne was at the helm, the fight for power between the Church, the King, and parliament raged. The parliament held a strong position because it controlled the success or failure of taxation and thereby the income of France. Jeanne hated the parliament and bore the brunt of the battle. Wars were brewing between France, England, Austria, Prussia, Russia, and Spain. France wanted free access from Louisiana to Canada and established forts along the Mississippi. England wanted to expand to the West and conflicts in the colonies became intense. France sent an expedition of 35 men to the colonies to negotiate with England. England sent 21 year old Major George Washington with 160 men and, when they met, Washington killed nearly all of the French "negotiators". There were fights on the seas and war was declared. European nations scurried for allies. The seven years war began.

While Louis busied himself with hunting and his little girls, the duc de Choiseul said Jeanne became "the arbitress of the destines of the Kingdom." Voltaire said: "Mademoiselle Poisson, dame Le Normand, Madame de Pompadour was, in fact, Prime Minister of the state."

The economies of France and England were being devastated by the war and both wanted peace.

Peace finally came and England was the biggest winner but France kept the West Indies, other territories, and a port in Africa that "was essential to the slave trade."

Jeanne's death came on April 15, 1764. She was 42 years and four months old. Voltaire said her death was "stoic and peaceful." He also said that "in her heart she was one of us" and "it is indeed ridiculous that an old scribbler is still alive and a beautiful woman should die while in the midst of the most dazzling career in the world."

What should we think of Jeanne? We can call her adulterous and a sinner; a woman who used sex and feminine charms to gain position, wealth, and power; a woman who condoned child abuse; and an unrepentant mistress. All of this is true but, in Jeanne's life, they were all means to accomplishments that lifted a nation to its zenith and helped save philosophy for future ages. Jeanne is just one of many women who changed the course of history.

A very different type of powerful women appeared on the stage of Western Civilization in the 1960s. (I will write in the present tense because I know nothing of the history of women that I write about since the 70s.) I am indebted to Barbara Decker for much of the following information.

Women like Kate Millett, Ti Grace Atkinson, Valerie Solonas, and Shulamith Firestone are direct, blunt, and deliberately crude in what they say. They want to offend and shock the general public and they do it well. On August 26, 1970, feminists, and a host of enlistees, parade their intentions and identify their targets when they stage a massive nationwide "women's strike for equality". They burn their bras in public. Large masses of professional women, students, housewives, artists, lawyers, and secretaries fill the streets carrying signs that say: "Don't cook dinner—starve a rat today"; "End human sacrifice—Don't get married". They make no bones about wanting to eradicate patriarchy and to do this they must eliminate the institution of traditional marriage. If a man and woman marry, or remain married, they want to eliminate patriarchy within the family by diminishing the power and value of the man in the family. They dwarf the role of fathers by pushing legislation that, act by act, places the family under rapidly increasing state dependency and control; and providing economic support to single mothers who remain unmarried.

I want to tell you about two distinctly different types of feminists. The types are different primarily in their perceptions of, and attitudes toward, men. One type sees the generic man as primarily a competitor and displays predominant attitudes of mistrust and antipathy toward him. The other type sees the generic man as primarily as potential friends who can cooperate and help her accomplish her wishes. Both types are feminists but the first type tends to be radical feminists with strong liberal political leanings. The first type is also more vociferous and demonstrative and has produced the most drastic changes in Western Societies. The second type tends to be more conservative and traditional but still wants women to be free and to fulfill their ambitions and potentials.

Beginning in the 1960s, both kinds of feminists start a revolution that achieves remarkable advances for women and makes the playing fields much more level for the genders. Feminists address genuine factual grievances of women. They take the initiative that lifts women to a much more equal status with men in politics, career opportunities, education, and positions of power in our most important institutions. Women have valid reasons to complain and their complaints are loud and effective. They fight for change and shake up the establishment in a way that transforms American society. (I have said in many public gatherings that women who gain power are the strongest civilizing force in any human society and will be the most decisive factor in ultimately achieving, or failing to achieve, a higher and better universal civilization. Islam nations will never be fully civilized until women liberate themselves. If they wait for patriarchs to do it for them, it will never be done. This does not relieve men of responsibility because women cannot do it alone; they must have men's cooperation.)

I will tell you about the two women who, I believe, best represent two types of feminists; Germaine Greer and Kate Millett. One brand of feminists excels in energizing and activating the women's movement and says "damn the torpedoes"; the other brand excels in rational arguments that say: "No one wins in a war."

Germaine

Germaine likes men. She is a good looking red head feminist from Australia who is full of fire and spirit, naturally rebellious, and bows to no one. It is hard for any man to not like and admire her unless he is a wimp and is threatened by her proud assertive spirit. Germaine immodestly asserts that she likes men and experiences great pleasure and satisfaction in sex with them. She mocks feminists who tout masturbation or sex with another woman as superior to sex with a man. She demonstrated in her life her fondness for men and her enjoyment of the heterosexual embrace.

In April of 1971, Germaine calls herself a late-starter in feminism but quickly makes up for lost time. She passionately wants to see women improve their lot and empower themselves and she links arms with women who are actively challenging the prevailing dominance of men in public positions of power. She shows women the folly of waiting on men to change the status-quo for them. She tells women that no one voluntarily gives up a position of power. Germaine detests weakness and passivity in men <u>and women</u>. She is powerful; a heroine; and a brilliant thinker.

In some ways, Germaine is out of step with most of her sisters. She has no intention of denigrating men or sexual relationships with men. Her affinity for men sways her ideas and there is a deep divide between her and feminists who, possessed by an abysmal opinion of the generic man, savage all men with pen, tongue, and deed. When her most important book, *The Female Eunuch*, is published in 1970, she lampoons women who castrate themselves and make themselves impotent and helpless. She scolds women who shirk responsibility by fleeing into a victim status. She sees how the role of victim is becoming politically powerfully and correct. To Germaine, weak, subservient, masochistic, and complaining women are pathetic creatures who wallow in the victim status and try to blame all of their impotence on men. She wants women to grow up and take responsibility for their happiness, status, and satisfaction—or the lack of it. When Anne Koedt ridicules men as clumsy and unsatisfying sex partners, Germaine replies: "One wonders just who Miss Koedt has gone to bed with."

Germaine agrees with her sisters when they attack marriage but she makes a distinction between a good marriage of equals and a marriage that promotes infantile dependency with the woman in a subservient role. She describes religiously sanctioned male domination and the temptations of immaturity in the "Holy Family" and says that if the "Holy Family" has to go, so be it. Like Shakespeare's Kate, she knows it takes a strong man to be a good husband to a strong woman, and vice versa. She wants marriage to be like her; full of fire.

We find in Germaine none of the rejection and disdain of marriage that is preached by many of her sisters. Feminists are effectively denouncing patriarchy as their worst enemy and squarely placing blame on it for inequality. Their mantra is that marriage makes patriarchy possible; therefore, women must end marriage to stamp our patriarchy. Germaine fights patriarchy but hold on to her man. She does not join the chorus that calls men beasts, rats, and rapists. Germaine likes men.

Germaine is "made to order" for the feminists revolution. She eagerly implants her aggressive spirit in the feminist movement and applauds women who are standing up for themselves and fiercely fighting for recognition and treatment as men's equal. She has no use for pansies or weakness or complaining in either gender. However, she does not like the hatred some radical women flaunt against men and the aggressive slogans that identify men as their enemy. She wants women to compete but believes they must also gain the cooperation of men to achieve their goals. "How", she asks, "do weak, dependent, and impotent women lift themselves by shifting responsibility for their sorry condition onto men?" She predicts that socially costly casualties will be an inevitable consequence of the foolish tactic of a hot angry "war against men". She warns feminists that no one wins in a war.

Kate

Kate Millet is the antipode to Germaine. She is a strong feminist leader, a heroine, and a highly intelligent influential author with a low opinion of the generic man. She set the movement on fire with her passion and strong blunt arguments. Kate is a physically attractive woman who can have men if she wants them but considers the generic man a first cousin to a Cretan. Kate is, I believe, bisexual and lives with a Japanese sculptor, Fumio Yoshimura. Neither wants marriage or children. In 1970, lesbian feminists create heated divisions in the women's movement by fighting for full and open acceptance in the National Organization of Women. Lesbian Rita Mae Brown resigns from NOW saying: "Lesbianism is the one word that gives the New York NOW Executive Committee a collective heart attack." Kate announces at the second Congress to Unite Women that she is bisexual (or lesbian) and the crowd explodes with loud applause. Her powerful influence turns the tide in favor of full inclusion of lesbians by NOW. This enhances her status as a recognized leader whose ideas are more war like, and perhaps more influential, than those of Betty Friedan; author of *The Feminine Mystique*.

When Kate publishes her book, *Sexual Politics*, in 1969, it becomes the Bible of radical feminists. In it, she creates mantras about men, marriage, and the family that starts a tidal wave of social change. Her ideas strongly sway judicial decisions in the highest and lowest courts; legislation on all levels of government; and the radical feminist and liberal bias of most teachers, business women and psychotherapists pouring out of liberal colleges. Her mantras, along with the teaching of liberal behavioral psychologist, are planted in the minds of students from kindergarten to post graduate education and soon become dominate in the most important politically correct institutions. She leads the nation in establishing governmental programs and funding for women's organizations and laws for female equality. She is a heroine of the largest segment of radical modern feminism.

Kate's believes men have women in a strangle hold that renders them helpless. She places blame for nearly all female ills squarely at the doorsteps of traditional patriarchy. She portrays women as defenseless because men have such huge economic and political advantages and they use their advantages to abuse, oppress, and rape women on a horrendous scale. She squarely endorses and promotes the victim status of women and makes sexual harassment charges a powerful political instrument.

She is in the forefront of the feminist blitzkrieg in the 1960s and 70s, waging war against male domination, patriarchy, inequality and marriage. (In 2009, it may be difficult for us to grasp the reality and seriousness of the announced intentions and clearly stated goals of early radical feminists. The successes of their movement and achievement of their intentions are now documented in demographic and social statistics.)

Radical feminist organizations flaunt their anger and aggression to garner as much attention as possible. They show an eagerness for combat that General Patton could admire. One group calls themselves WITCH (Women's International Conspiracy from Hell). In 1968, the New York Covens of WITCH issues a leaflet that says: "WITCH lives and laughs in every woman. She is the free part of each of us, beneath the shy smiles, the acquiescence to absurd male domination . . . If you are a woman and look inside yourself, you are a WITCH. You make your own rules." It's no wonder that frightened men label them as bitches.

Valerie Solonas becomes a leader in an organization called SCUM (Society for Cutting Up Men) which, according to Germaine, "advocates the most shocking strategy for allowing women to move back to humanity—simply that they exterminate men."

Solonas demonstrates her seriousness when she waits in ambush with a gun in her hand for Andy Warhol and, when he is within a few feet of her, exterminates him with a fusillade of bullets. Roxanne Dunbar dons her recently purchased military fatigues and combat boots and leaves her husband and their year old baby to join a radical group and boast about being the first feminist to publically advocate masturbation as a substitute for having sex with men. Feminists picket the New York Marriage

License Bureau and hand out a leaflet which calls marriage a "slavery-like institution" and says: "We can't destroy the inequalities between men and women until we destroy marriage." A segment believes that all men are Cretan rapists and any act of penal penetration of a woman's vagina is rape.

Germaine and Kate demonstrate the key difference between the two brands of feminism; one perceives the generic man, with varying degrees of animosity, as their competing foe; one perceives the generic man, with varying degrees of friendly acceptance, as their potential cooperating ally who can help women lift themselves out of inequality.

Consequences

How well did feminists succeed in fighting for the advancement of women? Female students now outnumber male students in colleges and universities. Women can now engage in every sport than a man can, except football. A large majority of colleges and universities are dominated by liberal, politically correct faculties with feminist professors. Your family physician and lawyer is just as likely to be female as male—and more likely in some places.

How successful have the radical feminists' attacks on traditional marriages been? Here is one example. In 2000, the number of fatherless children in black families had risen to 60%. That number is now 70%. The breakdown of the black family has contributed more than anything else to black poverty—the same is true of poor white fatherless families. I am now asserting that two of the worst enemies of the black race in America are the family destroying work of radical feminists and the Government's programs that aided, abetted, and encouraged the unfortunate phenomena of unwed and single moms.

I do not limit a good marriage to a man and woman with a legal marriage license. A good strong and lasting pair bond between two adults (preferably male and female) that works well for both partners and helps them give good quality care to their children (if they have children) is my idea of a good genuine marriage.

I don't know if marriage was given a knockout blow by radical feminists, but it is reeling. I don't know what portion of credit or blame to give radical feminists for the dramatic changes in America families since the 1960s, but the trend is certainly what they said they wanted. In 1960,

8.2% of all American families with children under 18 were headed by single parents; in 1970, the percentage was 11.8; in 1980 it was 19.2%, in 1990 it was 23.7 %; and in 2000 it was 27.1%. Parental authority and responsibility isn't even close to what it was in 1960. These are intentional consequences of the gender war. In the remaining two parent families with children, large portions of parental authority have been transferred to, or proscribed by, the State. Ozzie and Harriet families have gone the way of the dinosaurs.

Women also still carry nearly all the load of caring for and teaching our children, as they have from the beginning of time. Far more women than ever are now Governors of States, Mayors of cities, Senators, Congresswomen, and CEOs of large corporations. Our economy would collapse tomorrow if all women stopped working outside of the home. Our military forces could not survive without them. Women have enlisted more men in more care and responsibility for the young, but women will probably always provide the lion's share.

I hope the prevailing perceptions of radical feminists are becoming less hostile to traditional men and families. I hope the natural conflicts of interests between the genders are becoming better understood and pair bonds that last and work make the interests of their children their primary interest. Nature invented the human pair bond primarily in the interest of the young and is a major reason why our species survived and became successful. The ladies will call the shots about marriage and I'm putting my hopes for our future on the ladies.

We think that the cave man used social tactics much like those of baboons. The alpha males ruled all subordinate males and females. We know that Oriental emperors and kings monopolized thousands of wives and concubines employing the tactics of a tyrant. But this kind of domination of women made women in Western Civilizations "mad as hell and they decided they would not take it anymore." Will Islam women ever throw off the yoke of domineering patriarchy? I hope and believe that we can see signs of women in Islam cultures beginning to fight for more freedom and equality.

Even today, the pair bond has a good chance of working and lasting if both husband and wife have goals and can help each other reach their goal. The odds for a good lasting pair bond can rise dramatically if they have a common goal and know they are working together to accomplish it. The goal can be raising children or something else but they realize they need each other. Who needs to be the boss? That is a silly question. Both need to be the boss at different times and in different ways that both understand and accept.

Radical feminists have gained new freedoms for women while damaging different freedoms. Many more women work outside the home. This was going to happen with or without feminists. A working woman, who faces the choice of remaining with an asshole husband or becoming a single mom with little, or no, relatives around to help, can only choose between bad and worse. Many women, who work outside the home, want to be at home with their kids but must work because they provide the only income. Women are often torn between wanting to be at work and wanting to be at home with the kids.

Feminists rightly deserve tremendous credit, and some blame, for many dramatic social changes since the 1950s. I hope I am wrong by stating that the feminists' part of the responsibility for single moms and fatherless children makes them one of the worst enemies of the black race; but I am afraid that I am not wrong. I say that also because of feminists' power in bending our important institutions and government in the direction of socialism, and influencing the thinking and behaviors of men and women. Patriarchy can be bad; it can sometimes be real bad; but so can fatherless children.

CHAPTER SEVENTEEN

MYTHS AND CONS

A week of two ago, a television anchor talked, about Lincoln's Emancipation Proclamation and used these words. She called Lincoln the "Great Emancipator" and said his Proclamation "freed millions of slaves." She was terribly mistaken, just like practically all people who heard her. Most people in the nation take what she said for granted and believe her words were factual. If we know the actual facts about Lincoln and his partial Emancipation, we know Lincoln was <u>not</u> and never intended to be, the Great Emancipator of American slaves. Millions of slaves were <u>not</u> set free by Lincoln's Emancipation Proclamation. The, now hallowed but false, belief is one of the worst cons perpetrated on the black race. Lincoln's Proclamation did not emancipate slaves in States that were loyal to the Union and could not touch slaves in Confederate States. The strongest wish of Lincoln was to colonize all blacks and see them move out of the nation. The legal status of all American slaves was changed from slave to free by later constitutional amendments.

I have documented myths that have been morphed into distorted history and gross prejudice toward Southern States and people. Sometimes it hurts to hear the badly misinformed prejudice against my family, but what I wish for, more than anyone else, is for black people to see the cons that exploit their race. I have the crazy notion that the truth can do more to set all men free than false information and beliefs fostered by biased myths. I want black people to know the truth about prejudice and racism and the methods used to stereotype and stigmatize them; and I want them to recognize phony friends and real enemies of their freedom and upward mobility. You, my black friends, were injured far more than anyone else by the Civil War, the Congressional Reconstruction, and the still raging political wars.

I have described and explained how the politically correct culture championed by radical feminists and others injures black families; the actual war against black men that imprisons and stigmatizes them; and the socialist leaning programs that enslave black and white poor people with a bondage that is veiled and deceptive. Racism and prejudice are still the sly and efficient political tools of opportunists that exploit the underclass with phony promises and incite class and racial warfare. This includes greedy tenement land lords, the justice bureaucracy, do-gooders, civil rights leaders, religious leaders, failed schools, blatant exploiters of the most vulnerable, and, especially, the occupants of seats in Congress and the Oval Office.

I seldom, if ever, hear a sermon in a white church that exposes and explains prejudice, racism and today's bondage of black people? (I must admit that I now seldom go to church.) Few, if any, pastors tell their audience that all of them harbor some measure of prejudice and racism within them? Whether or not they believe it; it's a fact. It resides in all of us and denial makes honest efforts to reduce malignant prejudice more difficult. We can parse words to deny the existence of prejudice and racism; but it is everywhere and, the crucial question is: "What are we going to do with it?"

A successful pastor preaches to the choir and tells his congregation what he knows they want to hear. Do the opposite and you are kicked out. Many people may be offended if a pastor tells them that they are in some ways, and to some degree, prejudiced and racist. Pastors must not go too far out on a limb because churches have budgets and bills to pay After all, the Good Book did say that slaves should submit to their masters (and wives to their husbands). What kind of fool would tell his congregation that they are prejudiced—even if he had a way of knowing that it was true?

Should we listen to black leaders like Reverends Wright and Farrakhan? The answer is: "yes"; we should listen to them to learn about black emotions and problems. The answer is: "no"; we cannot listen to them to find solutions to racial problems; unless we agree with the Nation of Islam that the black race should be totally and permanently separated from the white race. I heard divisive prejudice and racism in two sentences spoken by Rev. Wright. He must think that racial animosity in America is too feeble and he needs to put more muscles on its bones. He gets cheers and creates bonds in his congregation by giving them a common enemy in the white race. The black race has legitimate grievances but must the white race be an enemy of black people? How is anyone helped by exacerbating racial tension and hostility?

Did the Union victory in the civil war guarantee a fair shake for the black race in America? Did it remove their social and economic disadvantages? The Congressional Reconstruction hurt many more black people than it helped. When the Union troops and carpet baggers returned home ten years after the war, preferential treatment for black people disappeared. The odds favoring social and economic upward mobility for most black people also tanked, along with fair and equal justice for all people accused of a crime. What do the prison populations, black poverty, and big city slums tell us? The mystery is not the fact that many black people have been hamstrung because of their race; the mystery is how have black men and women been able to overcome disadvantages, as individuals and a race, to climb so far so fast. Many individual black men and women have achieved remarkable success in business, the professions, government, and academia. The success and domination of black men in professional football, basketball, and other sports has been overwhelming and black entertainers are molding the culture of young people of all races.

Blacks suffered in all of the States but they wanted to stay in America—and they did. The black race is now a permanent and vital part of our nation's population and our political and social landscape. But, as a race, black people are still not as free as the white race and if we do not work toward that goal, all races will fall short of the best that they can be. Our welfare is directly linked to theirs. We must become as color blind as possible and respect the different cultures of all races; and still find a way to be one nation.

To Socrates, the most essential knowledge that people should seek is knowledge of one's own self. The search for knowledge and wisdom should begin with a person's honest examination of herself or himself, and an honest examination must include the best and worst in us. There is no real understanding of mankind until the mind turns round and examines itself. "*Gnothi seauton*," said Socrates: Know thyself. This is a strong admonition and it is a yoke of stringent demands on all philosophers, students, teachers, and anyone who wants to be free from pernicious prejudice. His first assignment for Socratic thinking was for a person to use it on himself or herself. The person must ask, and try to honestly answer, critical and searching personal questions. How can we understand someone else if we do not know ourselves? How can we understand prejudice if we cannot see it in our own heart? Our worst cons are on ourselves.

> "What makes me like I am?"
> These desires and fears and forbidden thoughts.
> Why do they come?
> Do I will them? Do they come by their own accord?"

> These things I do;
> So often vain; So often I regret;
> Why?
> Is it me or something within me with power of its own?"

> "My best and worst;
> My strengths and weaknesses;
> Virtues and faults,
> Lowest and highest,
> All that I really am;
> Do I truly want to know?"
> "Am I afraid to know?"
> And prefer to just pretend?"

> Bob

Are you and I God? If we engage in way-out abstract thinking, we can imagine the case. Are you and I one with all existence? If all existence really did come from one big bang, then I guess we could all be part of one event and one existence. If there is something in us, or about us, that is indestructible, I guess that does make us Gods. If all of that was true, what difference would it make in our everyday living? Isn't it hard enough to be a human without worrying about being a God?

Mary Parent, my first and best therapist, looked straight into my eyes at the end of a session and said: "You really think you are God." I was shocked. She made the statement with no show of emotions and with no explanation. I was angry. I stewed about it all week. Me! God! That woman does not know how guilty I feel and how hard I try to be humble—how could she possibly think that I thought I was God? I was offended but I trusted Mary; I knew she would not say something like that just to anger and upset me.

It was hard for me to wait a week for our next session. When I saw her again, Mary helped me to understand how hard it was for me to know and understand myself as a human, and to accept myself as a human—with all of the flaws, warts, base thoughts and desires, envy, anger, jealousy, and all the rest that goes with the good of being human. Mary helped me a lot; at least in starting to work on learning how to understand and accept my human nature and allow myself to be human. I was in denial and repressing realities about myself as a human being. Denial and repression were my defenses against guilt and self-loathing. Mary was asking if I could see, acknowledge to myself, and come to terms with repressed realities about normal, basic, wishes, thoughts and emotions in myself as a human and that they are not in themselves good or evil but can be expressed in good or bad behavior.

I hope it is true that God is Love; and that Love is more powerful than negative force, coercion, intimidation, and seduction. I hope that Love is a power that prevails in human beings and, perhaps, some day in human societies. But, then I remember two people; Adam and Eve. And I remember choice and that there is no guarantee that man will make the right choices. Then I remember responsibility and consequences. It's not all that easy being human. It can be heaven or hell.

A majority of Americans now readily agree that the nation is headed in the wrong direction even though they don't have the foggiest idea about what direction we are headed in.

Many people believe that we need a drastic fundamental changes; something like a revolution. If we have a revolution, I hope it is not like the Los Angeles riots or the French Revolution. Too many people in this country are already losing their head. Having a revolution like that in this country would be like filling the hold of our wooden Ship of State with termites. If a revolution is the only way that the country can transcend black injustice and white poverty, then let it come. I am too old to fight; too poor for anyone to rob; and too senile to know which side I was on. I do hope that we will set our rudder and sails for more, rather than less, freedom.

Dreams of Utopia

Brothers and sisters: everyone?
Peace and harmony everywhere?
War and hate: forever gone?
Songs of compassion anointing the air?

Is it just a dream impossible?
A wish never fulfilled?
A summit we can never scale?
A perfection; far too ideal?

"Why try?" The cynic and hopeless cry?
"Because we're human," the wise reply.
And human beings never fail,
On earth to create heaven and hell.

"So why, with toil and tears do we try,
To reach an unreachable goal?"
"Because we're human," the hopeful reply.
With the will to reach higher in good men's souls.
                                        Bob

People with goodwill and without pernicious prejudice and racism are more interested in healing and promoting friendly relationships than assigning blame and I am defending the South from unjust and unwarranted blame. The scars of the 1800s remain and some wounds will not heal. Perhaps the ghosts may eventually disappear but only if myths are dispelled. I sincerely believe that I had rather help people than harm them and that will be enough to get me through the bad.

CONCLUSION

I hope the reader has seen the similarities between troubling circumstances in our nation today and the political and emotional circumstances before, during, and after the Civil War. Please do not think that I am suggesting—or even hinting—that our nation is in foreseeable danger of the mass conflagration that erupted openly in 1961. However, we face similar tensions and conflicts today in divisive and hostile politics and media influences on common people. The central disagreement then and now is between State rights and freedom and Federal power and control. Both Lincoln and Davis truly believed they were acting in their own, and their nations, best interest. I hope you will accept as a given that the bottom cause of the Civil War was no different than the cause of all wars; fighting for power, control, booty, and territory by whatever means may work. I also hope there is no need to prove that violence always rears its bloody ugly head when divisions, conflicts, and passions become too hot and greedy. Winning elections is the name of the game. I have the word of Mr. Gallup and other trustworthy pole gurus that most people are mad as hell at our government today. Some nuts have already committed violence. Are there lessons that we can learn from the Civil War that can help us?

I want you to know that I am proud of my Southern heritage and family. And I hope you can believe that my maternal grandmother is a fair representation of poor white people in the 1800s. No one could know my grandmother without respecting her. She is the only grandparent that I had a chance to know.

At the time of this writing, September, 2011, I am 86 years old. My mother was born in 1891 and lived to be 102 years old. Her mother was born in Mississippi in 1855. My grandmother lived in my home during the last nine years of her life and died in my home. My grandmother experienced and witnessed the Civil War and the Congressional Reconstruction era. Even though she suffered a slow painful death from a cancer, I never heard her complain and I often think of her when I am writing

My grandmother grew up in a poor home and was the oldest of several children. When her mother died she took the roll of mother and became the primary caregiver for her younger siblings and had to delay her marriage. When her first husband died she was left with two small children, no income, no public welfare, and no place to live. A kind farmer let my grandmother live in a barn with a dirt floor that was close to his house and provided enough food for them to survive. She worked in the fields to do what she could to repay the farmer for his kindness.

A Confederate veteran heard about my grandmother and came to see her and, as a Southern gentleman should, came with personal references in his hand. He was older than my grandmother and a widower. His children were old enough to be mostly on their own. He asked my grandmother if she would marry him and let him help her raise her children. He promised to be good to her and her children. My grandmother told him she could not love him as she did her first husband but she would marry him and be a good wife to him if he would promise to never raise a hand against her children. My mother often said she could not have had a kinder and better father. He made it possible for my mother to go to a teacher's college and teach in a one room schoolhouse until she married my father.

My grandmother never attended school but taught herself to read. She experienced the harsh conditions in the South during the war and "reconstruction" and heard her second husband talk about his experiences during the fighting. She had good reasons to loathe Abraham Lincoln.

How could she not loathe him? She rightly blamed Lincoln for the war and devastation of the South. She also blamed Lincoln for the punitive treatment of the South during reconstruction. Her feelings toward Lincoln may have softened a bit if she could have known that Lincoln wanted healing and reconciliation for the South and opposed the radicals' harsh treatment of formerly seceded States. I wish that she could have known that during the short time that Lincoln lived after the war, he fought radical Congressmen's intentions to punish the South. My grandmother and my mother were Epicurean enough to enjoy simple pleasures and were Stoic in the highest and best meaning of the word. My wife is cut from the same cloth and that is one of many reasons why I love her so much.

I believe Lincoln made a tragic mistake when he made the decision to go to war. I believe the American Civil War was the worst travesty in American history. I have given reasons in the text for my belief. We can never know what our country would be like today if the South was allowed to secede. I hope that we will fight our second Civil War with much more civility and much less harm to people. I hope my writing sheds a little light on the way that unique mistreatment of black people has become institutionalized and how prejudice and racism remains a serious problem that makes good relationships more difficult; perhaps impossible. We are not divided now by sectional differences as much as we are by ideology and politics.

I may be an incurable foolish romantic but I believe Love is a power stronger than force, coercion, or intimidation. I believe that Love is more powerful than hate and hostility. I also believe wise self-interest with good will is another way of describing Love. Factually, the world is rapidly becoming "one" in commerce, communication, and interdependent in ways that make reliance on force too foolish and dangerous for any sane person or nation. I believe that our future can be hopeful and promising if wise leaders realize the stupidity and potential horrors of misused force. Homo-sapiens have no guarantee that we will not go the way of the dinosaurs.

There is still that matter of choice. Make your choice and stake your life on it. The only thing that you have to lose is all of your tomorrows.

POST OPINION AND VENTILATION

Goons fight by spreading propaganda and smearing their opponents with dishonest crap. They use freakish television knuckleheads and other prostituted megaphones of the media to excrete sneaky political prejudice, racism, and bias. These radio and television exhibitionists love to invent and exaggerate nasty fights. They specialize in exacerbating conflicts between different sections, personalities, and parties. They love to smear their opposition with vile rumors, half truths and whole lies. Unfortunately, many of these self serving nitwits and shallow purveyors of false information have a wide audience and are the primary sources of "news" and "information" for many people. The saddest part of the story is that many human beings are ridiculously easy to indoctrinate and swallow their garbage like silly geese; especially when they hear what they want to hear.

Three, of the numerous prolific television entertainers posing as news casters and commentators, are the lucky recipients of my attention. They are examples of others like them. They are Chris Matthews, Sean Hannity, and Bill Maher. They are specimens of the shallow bellowing of commercially motivated bias, prejudice, and denigration of everyone who does not agree with their political ideology. I choose these lucky three because their bias and concrete thinking are, to me, so obvious and their audiences are large.

Chris is a clear darling of the left; Sean is a golden boy of the right; and Bill is the reigning champion of sarcasm about religion, republicans, and Southerners and is clearly obsessed with the f word. Chris revels in contemptuous ridicule of Sarah Palin, George Bush, "Red Necks, the "good old boys" in the South (that he believes still walk with their knuckles dragging the ground), the tea party, and stinking republicans. I think of him as the King of the Smirk. Sean revels in contemptuous ridicule of democrats, liberals, Hollywood, and President Obama. He is so sure of himself I think of him as the King of all Gigantic Egos. No one's ego is more inflated than Sean's except Bill O'Reilly's. I think of Bill O'Reilly as the Pope of Pious Self-appointed Moralists—but he makes at least a half-hearted attempt to be free of political bias. Bill Maher excels in his contempt for the Bible, "Jesus Freaks", Southerners, religion, and conservative kooks. I call him Mr. Sewer Mouth. No one, except stand up comics, spread more filth. I find all three of them bluntly prejudiced with narrow gauge one track minds.

Bill Maher bothers me the most because he sometimes makes good sense and he seems to lean toward Libertarians. It annoys the hell out of me when I find myself agreeing with some of the things that Bill says because his prejudice and ignorance about religion reveals the intelligence of a half-witted mule. He actually believes that he has made the astounding discovery that the story of Noah's ark may not be literal fact. What a mind! That discovery must have required many years of deep profound thinking and stringent research. No one could have thought of that possibility before you, Bill.

This book is not about God or religion but I must rebut Bill. You say that religion is the cause of all human ills and the sooner we get rid of it, the better. The major problems in modern religions are fanatics and extremists. If you will specify that you are opposed to fanatics and extremists, I will be on your side. I agree that there may never be an end to the hateful fights and bloody wars that they instigate.

Religion may sometimes be a necessary evil, but it has been necessary to every supposedly civilized culture, society, and nation in human history. Can you, Bill, cite one human social group in all of our hominid history that did not have a religion? It might be possible to name an individual but not a whole society. Even the Nazis had a religion.

Perhaps you believe that our Civil War merits your praise. If you do, you will have to give religion credit for their part in the war. Many of the most zealous abolitionists were staunchly religious. Some of the loudest advocates for abolition were pastors of Methodist churches in the 1800s. If you believe that our civil war was an avoidable travesty, you have another reason to attack religion. If you believe the war was necessary and worth the cost, you have a reason to praise religion.

Actually Bill, a simple fact is that you and I would not be here today if there had been no religion or church. Without social groups, we would have no civilization, and we would have no human social groups without bonds of common beliefs, traditions, and rituals; and nothing has provided that glue better than religions. The oldest common beliefs of different religions have been riddled with superstition but they provided the necessary glue.

No one can prove the existence of God. That's true. No one can prove that God does not exist. That is also true. It is also true that no one can explain why the universe exists—and why there is the existence of something instead of nothing. That leaves us with simple choices, Bill; to believe or not believe, and the choices have nothing to do with intelligence or stupidity. Both brilliant and stupid people choose to believe or not believe in the existence of a God. Agnostics make neither choice. Don't confuse choice with faith because they are not the same. What people believe <u>about</u> God is a matter of faith. It requires faith to believe that God is Love and that faith is hard. The suffering of so many people in the world, and sometimes our own suffering, can make faith in a loving God real hard to hold on to. People see their God differently. I understand religion as essentially a chosen path; the way of life that a person chooses and lives. You have a religion, Bill, unless you have made no choice in your way of life and have no point or purpose for your life. Your purpose, Bill, may be to make people laugh. That's fine, only in your case I do not know if the means justifies the end.

The three of you remind me of a corny old story. Three men were arguing about who was the most macho and who could endure for the longest time an extremely painful situation. A skunk was in a nearby chicken house and they began a contest to determine who could go in and remain with the skunk for the longest amount of time. Chris went in and after two minutes came running out with his eyes watering and unable to breathe. Sean went in with the same results. When you went in, Bill, the skunk immediately came running out.

I hope the clowns that I write about do not have as much influence as I think they have.

At times I listen to all three of them. I hope they cannot make us too pessimistic about our nation. For many years my favorite plaque hung in my office where I saw people for psychotherapy. It had a picture of a squirrel hugging its big bushy tail on it and the quotation from Oscar Wilde: "Life is much too important to be taken seriously." I needed that when I was listening hour after hour to depressed people. (I still see six people for therapy in my home office, but now, at age 86, they help me as much, or more, than I help them.)

I hope the Talking Heads and gloomy pessimists will never make us lose all faith in the common sense and trustworthiness of our fellow citizens, including people who stoutly disagree with us. We can lose faith in the Congress or the President but I do not believe that most ordinary

American citizens will always behave like ignorant, self-centered, irresponsible baboons. I criticize my country but I love it; and I still get goose bumps up and down my spine when I hear someone singing: "God bless America." I try to not let my ego get too involved in political squabbling. Meanwhile, talking heads will keep creating villains to vilify and scintillating sins, and doomsdays to stir irrational emotions in their voyeuristic audiences (like me). They will daily open Pandora's Box to provide us with tons of sex, sex crimes, murderers, war, natural and manmade disasters, perversions, and nasty fights between individuals and between political parties. They know how to attract an audience.

BIBLIOGRAPHY

Anderson, Fred and Clayton, Andrew, *The Dominion of War*, Penguin Group Inc., 375 Hudson St., New York, New York, 10014 2005.

Berlin, Jean V. *A Confederate Nurse, The Edited Diary of Ada W. Bacot*, University of South Carolina Press, 1994.

Bynum, Victoria, *The Long Shadow of the Civil War*, University of North Carolina Press, Chapel Hill, NC, 2010.

Crichton, Judy, *America 1900*, Henry Holt & Company, Inc., 115 West 18th Street, New York, NY, 10011.

Davis, William C., *Look Away*: a History of the Confederate States of America, The Free Press, 1230 Avenue of the Americas, New York, NY, 2002.

DiLorenzo, Thomas J., *The Real Lincoln* Prima Publishing, Roseville, California, 2002.

Goodwin, Doris Kearns, *Team of Rivals*, Simon & Schuster Paperbacks, 1230 Avenue of the Americas, New York, NY 10020, 2005.

Hyde, William De Witt, *Five Great Philosophies of Life*, The Macmillan Co., New York, NY, 1932.

Kennedy, Roger G., *Burr, Hamilton, and Jefferson,* Oxford University Press, 198 Madison Ave., New York, New York, 2000.

Lowry, Thomas P. M.D.,*The Story The Soldiers Wouldn't Tell*, Stackpole Books, 5067 Ritter Road, Mechanicsburg, PA, 1994.

McClintock, Russsell, *Lincoln and The Decision for War*, The University of North Carolina Press, Chapel Hill, NC, 2008.

Pollard, E. A., *The Lost Cause*, E. B. Treat and Company, New York, 1867

Rubin, Anne Sarah, *A Shattered Nation: The Rise and Fall of the Confederacy*, The University of North Carolina Press, Chapel Hills, North Carolina, 2005.

Sefton, James E., *Andrew Johnson and the Uses of Constitutional Power*, Little, Brown & Company, Limited, Canada, 1960.

Smith, Jean Edward, *Grant*, Simon & Schuster 1230 Avenue of the Americas, New York, NY, 10020, 2001.

Sandburg, Carl, *Abraham Lincoln*, Galahad Books, 386 Park Avenue South, New York, NY, 10016, 1966.

Stowe, Harriet Beecher, *Uncle Tom's Cabin*, John P. Jewett @ Co., Boston, 1852.

Thomas, Benjamin P., *Abraham Lincoln*, Barnes & Noble Books, New York, NY, 1952.

Trefousse, Hans L., *Rutherford B. Hayes*, Times Books, Henry Holt and Company LLC 115 W 18th St 10011 c 2002.

Trefousse, Hans L., *Andrew Johnson*, W. W. Norton & Company, Inc., 500 Fifth Avenue, New York, NY, 10110 1989.

Wiley, Irvin Bell, *Confederate Women*, Greenwood Press, 51 Riverside Ave., Westport, Connecticut, 1975

Wills, Garry, *James Madison*, Times Books, Henry Holt & Co., New York, NY, 115 Qwest 18th St., New York, NY, 10011, 2002.

Yarbrough, Jean M., *American Virtues: Thomas Jefferson on the Character of a Free People*, University Press of Kansas, Lawrence, Kansas, 1998.

Zakaria, Fareed, *The Future of Freedom*, W. W. Norton & Company, 500 Fifth Avenue, New York, NY, 10110.